Teaching Rhythmic Gymnastics

A Developmentally Appropriate Approach

Heather C. Palmer

Human Kinetics

Library of Congress Cataloging-in-Publication Data

Palmer, Heather C., 1961-
  Teaching rhythmic gymnastics : a developmentally appropriate approach
/ Heather C. Palmer.
     p. cm.
  ISBN 0-7360-4242-3 (softcover)
  1. Rhythmic gymnastics—Study and teaching (Elementary) 2. Rhythmic
gymnastics—Study and teaching (Secondary) I. Title.
  GV463 .P25 2003
  796.44—dc21

                                  2002152891

ISBN: 0-7360-4242-3

Acquisitions Editor: Judy Patterson Wright, PhD
Managing Editor: Jennifer L. Davis
Copyeditor: D.K. Bihler
Proofreader: Kathy Bennett
Graphic Designer: Fred Starbird
Graphic Artist: Angela K. Snyder
Photo Manager: Leslie A. Woodrum
Cover Designer: Andrew Tietz
Photographer (cover): Helen Scott Studios
Photographer (interior): Human Kinetics, except where otherwise noted
Art Manager: Kelly Hendren
Illustrator: Roberto Sabas
Printer: Versa

Printed in the United States of America   10 9 8 7 6 5 4 3 2 1

Human Kinetics
Web site: www.HumanKinetics.com

United States: Human Kinetics
P.O. Box 5076
Champaign, IL 61825-5076
800-747-4457
e-mail: humank@hkusa.com

Canada: Human Kinetics
475 Devonshire Road Unit 100
Windsor, ON N8Y 2L5
800-465-7301 (in Canada only)
e-mail: orders@hkcanada.com

Europe: Human Kinetics
107 Bradford Road
Stanningley
Leeds LS28 6AT, United Kingdom
+44 (0) 113 255 5665
e-mail: hk@hkeurope.com

Australia: Human Kinetics
57A Price Avenue
Lower Mitcham, South Australia 5062
08 8277 1555
e-mail: liahka@senet.com.au

New Zealand: Human Kinetics
P.O. Box 105-231, Auckland Central
09-523-3462
e-mail: hkp@ihug.co.nz

Acknowledgments

I would like to thank the teachers who, during my childhood, helped me find my path in life. Mr. Burt and Mrs. Davies ran an after-school gym club at Captain John Palliser School and introduced me to the sport of gymnastics. I am eternally grateful, for my successful beginning at a young age led to a lifelong love of gymnastics. This love grew in leaps and bounds and led me to take coaching courses and classes.

My love of coaching children in gymnastics led to a career in teaching. Through teaching I met my husband. Brian Unterschultz, husband, father, teacher, and administrator, has been my greatest supporter. Thank you, Brian, for letting me talk about my ideas and for giving up family time so that I could realize this dream.

Thanks to my parents, Dave and Bernice, for supporting my involvement in sport as a child, whether it was gymnastics, skating, swimming, or skiing. They shared with me the value of lifelong involvement in sport and encouraged me to pursue all my dreams.

Sincere thanks are extended to Connie Sturgess who first introduced me to rhythmic gymnastics and generously shared her knowledge and love of the sport. Connie exemplifies how successful a school rhythmic gymnastics program can be with her outstanding physical education program at Dalhousie School. Connie was an early founder of the sport in Canada and has trained many coaches and teachers who have had such a positive impact on so many children.

The children I have taught over the past 20 years have taught me the most about myself, about the importance of personal success, and about the vast possibilities of the sport of rhythmic gymnastics. Their boundless energy and endless creativity continue to astound me. A special thanks is extended to the students of Hillhurst Community School and gymnasts of Rhythmics West Gymnastics Club of Calgary for their enthusiasm and unending patience. Thanks also to Mario Lam for assisting me with the section on the history of sport.

My children have been my inspiration for developing the content of this book. Their natural love of music and movement were evident when they were babies. Their desire to create innovative movements and move to music continues today. Their patience while posing as models for many of the illustrations was greatly appreciated. Thank you, Emily and Hannah, for sharing your love with me. May you sing and twirl your way through life.

Special thanks to Jennifer Davis of Human Kinetics for guiding me through the editing process of this book with humor and patience. To Judy Patterson Wright, thank you for realizing the need for this resource and helping to see it through to fruition.

My work with Rhythmic Gymnastics Alberta has allowed me to pursue projects near and dear to my heart. For many years we have realized the need for a teacher's book to bring rhythmic gymnastics into the schools in a meaningful and appropriate way. Thanks to the board members of Rhythmic Gymnastics Alberta for their support and encouragement of this project. To Barb Miller, Diane Gunn, and Kerry Louw, thank you for sharing your confidence in me to complete this book and for all that you have done and continue to do for the development of the sport.

Contents

Preface

Rhythmic gymnastics is a sport that brings the joy and excitement of activity, music, and movement to students. The opportunity to make a ribbon twirl and dance appeals to children and to the child in every one of us. Movement opportunities are endless, as children use their natural creativity and imagination to manipulate ribbons, balls, hoops, ropes, and scarves in fun and wonderful ways.

The sport of rhythmic gymnastics provides a safe and fun alternative to a traditional gymnastics program. Traditional gymnastics does not always accommodate the unique body types and varied abilities of every student. Rhythmic gymnastics, however, encourages every child, regardless of age, gender, or ability, to challenge themselves to create movements with the apparatus at their individual level. Also, most teachers do not have the qualifications or specific training to teach the more complex skills of artistic or acrobatic gymnastics. But every teacher can deliver a rhythmic program without specialized training.

The emphasis on safety and developmentally appropriate practice in a physical education setting has prompted many teachers to abandon some of the high-risk activities of traditional gymnastics. This trend has prompted many school boards and districts to ban traditional types of gymnastics equipment, such as springboards and mini trampolines. Thus, more and more educators are seeking new ideas to enhance and expand their gymnastics and dance units.

Few resources have been developed for the school-based instruction of rhythmic gymnastics, until now. This book was developed to lead the educator through the process of planning and implementing a developmentally appropriate rhythmic gymnastics program. The program enables individuals to work at their own level and ability. That is, students have the opportunity to develop their skills individually or work within a group to develop creative sequences and routines. Through this individualized approach, and with some simple equipment modifications or program adjustments, teachers can easily facilitate the inclusion of special needs populations. By providing opportunities for exploration, open-ended movements, and ongoing challenge, teachers can guide students to self-discovery within their individual capabilities.

Rhythmic gymnastics is easy to teach and fun for students. With the program presented in this book, students will discover amazing skills and rhythmic movements on their own. As educators, we simply need to facilitate this learning by providing students with opportunities to discover their bodies' capabilities. After developing movement and spatial awareness, students get the opportunity to use apparatus, discovering the fundamental movements and the vocabulary for each along the way. To expand their learning, students refine and expand their movements through a series of learning challenges. The culmination of the learning process occurs when students combine their newly discovered skills into sequences and routines.

The benefits of rhythmic gymnastics are many. The physical, cognitive, and emotional skills and tools developed in a rhythmic gymnastics program are key to a child's growth and development. Physical abilities are strengthened as students come to know how their bodies can move with each apparatus. For example, rhythmic gymnastics involves throwing, catching, hand-eye coordination, fitness, and locomotion skills. Mastery of these skills transfers well to skill demands of other sports.

Students also gain self-confidence and self-esteem. Because many of the skills are easy to perform and visually exciting, students immediately experience a high level of accomplishment when they first use a rhythmic gymnastics apparatus. The self-confidence and self-esteem that result are further expanded as students are challenged to expand their rhythmic gymnastics abilities with new skills, sequences, and routines. Sequences and routines also encourage creativity and individuality, allowing students the opportunity to work at their own level and, therefore, experience individual success.

Social skills are also enhanced through rhythmic gymnastics. In group activities students learn leadership and cooperation skills as they collaborate on routine building. They also learn problem solving as they think through activities that challenge them to be more creative and imaginative. Finally, incorporating music into the rhythmic gymnastics program develops musicality and promotes aesthetic understanding.

This book offers practical information on planning a rhythmic gymnastics program for students ages 5 to 11. With some adaptations and extension, the learning challenges could be presented as skills to older students (this applies to children approximately ages 12 and older). Educators of younger students new to rhythmic gymnastics (5 to approximately 8 years of age) start by focusing on discovery and exploration, rather than skill, first without apparatus and then with apparatus. Teachers with older students will want to proceed through the exploration stage as a review and then guide students in creating their own sequences and routines. To accommodate varied student needs, this book presents six stages of an educationally based rhythmic gymnastics learning continuum. (These six stages are outlined in chapter 3.) Where you begin on the continuum will depend on either the age or prior experience of your students. This developmental approach will help you to individualize your instruction to challenge all students.

How This Book Is Organized

The book is divided into two parts. Part I provides the background needed to begin a rhythmic gymnastics unit. Chapter 1 discusses the rationale for teaching rhythmic gymnastics and explains the sport, its history, and important safety information. Chapter 2 addresses the equipment needs of a rhythmic gymnastics program, including practical suggestions on making your own apparatus as well as suggestions for equipment storage, distribution, and maintenance. Chapter 3 explains the six stages of implementing a rhythmic gymnastics program, from introducing students to the sport to helping them create their own routines. The planning phase starts in chapter 4, including how to incorporate students' ideas into the program. Chapter 5 goes further into the planning process, explaining how to plan a rhythmic gymnastics lesson. In this chapter you will learn how to develop a quick, easy lesson plan by using a teacher-ready rhythmic gymnastics lesson plan form. Chapter 6 outlines strategies for class management and organization. The final chapter in part I, chapter 7, presents some basic music terminology, including explaining such musical terms as tempo, rhythm, and beat, and provides suggestions for music selection.

Part II presents ways to extend student learning through specific tasks, activities, and challenges. In chapter 8, the discussion focuses on spatial awareness and movement concepts (e.g., personal spatial awareness, direction, pathways, levels, planes). Body elements specific to rhythmic gymnastics (e.g., locomotion, jumps, leaps, balances, turns, pivots) are explained with supporting activities for each. Chapter 9 introduces rhythmic gymnastics movements with apparatus. (Note: Students should have prior movement experience before being introduced to specific apparatus.) Skill instruction is suggested for every fundamental movement for each apparatus: ribbon, hoop, ball, rope, and scarf. Within the ball section, for example, skill tasks are categorized under swings, circles, rolls (on the floor and on the body), bounces, figure 8s, and throws and catches. After exploring these movements for each apparatus, students will be able to connect the skills and move on to the fun and challenge of creating routines. Chapter 10 presents some ways to refine a rhythmic gymnastics program for older or more experienced students. This chapter delves deeper into routine creation and development, asking students to consider what constitutes a good routine and how to make a routine more interesting. This chapter also provides suggestions for choreography, assessment, and performance planning.

The book contains teaching tools useful in developing a rhythmic gymnastics unit. These convenient and time-saving tools include ready-to-use checklists, assessment guidelines, lesson plans, a routine-planning poster, and a word search worksheet for vocabulary development. In the appendix you will find routine charts that can be enlarged on a copier and posted in the gym.

Rhythmic gymnastics is an enjoyable sport that develops fitness, promotes creativity, and enables individuals to work at their own level. As such, it is an integral part of a high-quality physical education program. What is more, by affording students the opportunity to discover rhythmic gymnastics, nurture their own creativity, and exercise their imaginations, you will also learn from your students as they explore the infinite movements, combinations, and routines within the sport. My hope is that you and your students will discover the fun and joy of rhythmic gymnastics.

On a final note, learning a new subject or sport is a great way to inject energy and enthusiasm into your teaching. It is my hope that you will find this book helpful in discovering the sport of rhythmic gymnastics, that you will gain confidence in teaching rhythmic gymnastics, and that you will share your newfound knowledge and confidence with your colleagues and students. The sport has brought many opportunities my way for working with children in a fun and creative manner, and the rewards have been wonderful and numerous. Along the way many children have shared their appreciation and gratitude at being given the opportunity to be innovative and creative within a sport setting.

Chapter **1**

© Helen Scott Studios

Rhythmic Gymnastics

Rhythmic gymnastics is a sport that uses a hand apparatus in combination with varied body movements. Through exploration and discovery, children learn fun and interesting ways to use their bodies and manipulate ribbons, hoops, balls, scarves, and ropes. Once basic skills are learned, they can be linked together to form sequences. Sequences can then be linked together to form fun and interesting routines. The opportunities for creativity in movement and skill development with apparatus are endless.

The addition of music adds further enjoyment to the sport. Indeed, music is an integral component of a rhythmic gymnastics program. First, music makes the activity both captivating and fun. Second, music helps to inspire and guide the movement of both the gymnast and the apparatus. Music accompanies rhythmic gymnastics along the continuum, from stages of exploration and discovery to the performance of sequences and routines. During the discovery stage, music can be used to help guide the child's movement. If you put on marching music with a definite beat you will naturally elicit from the children a different response than if you put on a soft and flowing piece of music. When older students develop sequences and routines to music, they will likely choose music than suits their own personal style and taste. Their movement choices with the apparatus will be influenced by their chosen music. Music can inspire the movements and assist in the exploration and discovery process.

As a competitive sport, rhythmic gymnastics demands that athletes be strong and powerful yet flexible and agile. Within the competitive realm, rhythmic gymnasts are female and can compete as individuals or within a group of four to six gymnasts. The judged routines are guided by a code of points, requirements set by the Fédération Internationale de Gymnastique (International Gymnastics Federation, or FIG). Competitive rhythmic gymnasts must be highly motivated and willing to commit to a demanding practice and training schedule.

In stark contrast to the competitive realm is the school-based rhythmic gymnastics program, which focuses equally on social fun, active participation, and enjoyment. In the school setting, the sport is gender neutral and appeals to students of all ages and abilities. Students discover their abilities through movement and by manipulating apparatus. They learn the fundamental elements of and skills for working with each apparatus. Soon in the process they begin to discover that they have been doing rhythmic gymnastics from their early years, from the day they picked up their first ball and threw it into the air. When introducing the sport to students, I will often inquire, "Has anyone here ever skipped rope?" "Has anyone ever bounced a ball?" The unanimous response is, of course, yes. Indeed, although they may not know it, every student has had some experience with rhythmic gymnastics. Every hoop roll, ball bounce, or skipping step can be included under the umbrella of rhythmic gymnastics.

History of the Sport

The history of rhythmic gymnastics is rooted in European traditions and extends to the very beginning of the modern gymnastics. Rhythmic gymnastics grew out of the Swedish system of free exercise developed by Per Henrik Ling in the early 1800s. Ling's concept of aesthetic gymnastics encouraged students to express their feelings and emotions through fluid movements of the body in the form of mass exercise. Catherine E. Beecher extended Ling's concept into her own program called "grace without dancing," in which young women exercised to music with the goal of developing good health. In 1911, Emile Jaque-Dalcroze devised eurythmics, a system of rhythmic exercises set to music as a way to express musical rhythm. The Medau School of Berlin was established in 1929 to train new leaders about what was then called "modern gymnastics." At the same time, an emerging type of rhythmic gymnastics began to incorporate apparatus such as balls, clubs, ropes, and tambourines. The sport eventually progressed to include a competitive focus where specific skills were given a degree of difficulty. These founders of modern gymnastics, now rhythmic gymnastics, laid the foundation of the sport we know today.

FIG first recognized rhythmic gymnastics as a sport in 1962. The first world championships were held in 1964. Today the sport is flourishing in both the recreational and competitive realms and across many nations. Every four years the highlight for many gymnasts around the world is the World Gymnaestrada. A supportive and collegial gathering of gymnastics groups in a celebratory festival setting, the World Gymnaestrada is an event organized by FIG's General Gymnastics division to provide the opportunity for noncompetitive gymnasts to perform gymnastics simply for their own enjoyment and love of the sport. The word *gymnaestrada* is derived from the words *gymnae*, meaning "gymnastics," and *strada*, meaning "street."

The roots of the World Gymnaestrada can be traced to early European gymnastics festivals, which grew in size and popularity and eventually began to include other countries. The first Gymnaestrada took place in 1953 in Rotterdam, Netherlands. Once it was officially dubbed the World Gymnaestrada, the event was held in Amsterdam in 1991, then in Berlin in 1995. For the 1999 World Gymnaestrada, Göteborg, Sweden, hosted more than 21,000 participants from 40 nations. Lisbon, Portugal, will host the 2003 World Gymnaestrada. The success and popularity of the World Gymnaestrada is a testament of how people of all ages and across all nations love the sport of gymnastics.

Why Should We Teach Rhythmic Gymnastics?

Rhythmic gymnastics is a sport that ensures success for anyone who participates, regardless of age or ability. Students benefit physically and emotionally, and they have fun. Teachers can meet their curricular requirements in dance, games, fitness, creative movement, and gymnastics in a safe manner with a rhythmic gymnastics unit. Indeed, when simple safety precautions are heeded, rhythmic gymnastics is a safe form of gymnastics. The following sections outline some of the many benefits of a rhythmic gymnastics unit.

Health and Fitness

The smooth and flowing movements of rhythmic gymnastics often appear effortless, so it is easy to underestimate the value of the sport in developing physical fitness. When body movements with apparatus are combined with locomotion skills, the participant's heart rate quickly increases. Sustaining this higher level of intensity will develop cardiovascular fitness. Flexibility is developed through gentle stretching activities and by encouraging full range of motion in the joints. Muscle strength is developed through running and jumping activities and through apparatus manipulation. Try spiraling a ribbon for a full minute and you will begin to feel that all the arm's muscle groups are being utilized from wrist up to the shoulder. Balance is developed through the exploration of static positions and activities that encourage children to balance on different body parts. Hand-eye coordination is developed through the use of the small apparatus such as hoops, rope, ball, and scarves where the equipment is often thrown and retrieved as part of the activities and routines. Active participation in a rhythmic gymnastics program improves health and fitness and promotes an overall sense of wellness.

Musicality

The use of music in rhythmic gymnastics promotes musicality and self-expression. By selecting a variety of music, students are exposed to a wide range of music styles, which develops their knowledge of and appreciation for music. With the addition of movement, students are able to express themselves physically and often emotionally. In some ways this self-expression can help to relieve the stress today's youth experience in their busy lives. Rhythmic gymnastics offers them an opportunity to escape from the realities of their world, if only for a brief time, to find pleasure in music and movement.

Skill Transfer

Skills developed through rhythmic gymnastics, such as hand-eye coordination and body awareness, transfer well to other sports. To do well in rhythmic gymnastics, students must learn to move their arms and hands in coordination with other body parts. This learning process involves the entire body and the mind. As students' total body and spatial awareness improves, along with overall coordination, so will their skill level in other sports.

Self-Confidence and Self-Esteem

Strong self-esteem and self-confidence can be developed through rhythmic gymnastics. The novelty of the apparatus encourages many students who are otherwise inhibited to become more adventurous. For many, a natural curiosity leads them quickly into active participation. Many rhythmic gymnastics skills are easy to master; thus, participants experience success early on. And even the simplest skills are visually appealing and aesthetically pleasing. As soon as they pick up the apparatus, the results are immediate and positive. Even a slight flick of the wrist will result in an interesting pattern from the ribbon's movement. The results of working with rhythmic equipment are immediate and satisfying. Children quickly gain confidence in their abilities and consequently feel great about themselves as "gymnasts." Students with physical limitations can set realistic goals for themselves while enjoying the fun of the movement and the music. Physically talented children can challenge themselves to learn more advanced skills or to extend their ideas and create complex sequences and routines. All children regardless of their abilities will feel good about the wonderful movement patterns they can create in a rhythmic gymnastics program.

Social Interaction and Group Dynamics

Rhythmic gymnastics promotes social interaction and enhances group dynamics. Students learn to work together to create routines and sequences. They learn to cooperate and collaborate as they negotiate the creative process of routine building. For students who choose to include rhythmic gymnastics in their extracurricular activities and join a performing group or stay involved in the sport, the social benefits can last a lifetime.

Indeed, further involvement in the sport can lead to performances at festivals, halftime shows, the World Gymnaestrada, or other special events. In European countries, men and women practice and perform rhythmic gymnastics to improve fitness and promote relaxation and socialization. My own province in Canada once hosted a group of Danish youth who were part of a gymnastics performing group touring North America. I asked one of the female gymnasts, in her early 20s, why she has stayed involved in the sport. She smiled sweetly and, pointing behind her to a large group of male and female athletes, replied, "I like to spend time with people my own age and travel. We have so much fun together and I like to do gymnastics." For this young woman, rhythmic gymnastics has led to wonderful friendships, lifelong fitness, and international travel.

Goal Setting

Goal setting can become an integral part of the rhythmic gymnastics program. Students can set their own attainable goals within their own comfort levels. Such personal goal setting is important for self-evaluation purposes. Students can set goals that are personally relevant and suitable and strive to attain these goals by the end of a rhythmic gymnastics program. Goal setting may include learning new skills, wanting to teach a new skill to the class, or creating a routine with the required number of elements and then demonstrating it in front of a group. Evaluation of the goal is an important indicator of success, and will enable students to set further goals for their personal growth and development.

Brain Development

Today's educators are becoming increasingly aware of the need to understand the brain and its complex functions, and then use that knowledge to deliver effective educational programs. Research has identified that children learn best when instruction is active, connected, and cohesive. This is a far cry from the passive learning and rote memorization of yesterday. Students are now encouraged to talk about each task, to move while thinking, and to work collaboratively with others in a sharing, cooperative environment.

The depth of this relationship between physical activity and learning is just starting to be understood, but it is now widely accepted that children's brains are stimulated by physical activity. These thought patterns are particularly evident in gymnastics, where the brain is actively engaged in creating and performing smooth and flowing movements as well as problem solving and correction. In rhythmic gymnastics, which combines the movements and challenges of gymnastics with music—itself a wonderful sensory stimulus—students are truly engaging in active learning.

Those who regularly participate in physical activity already enjoy the benefits of fitness on their overall sense of well-being. Students participating in rhythmic gymnastics will also see these benefits early on, feeling euphoric and rejuvenated after a routine. The physical movements that cross over or pass through the visual midline assist the brain's integration of its two hemispheres. When the left side of the body is used along with the right side, the brain must communicate between the two hemispheres. The most basic example of this movement is described throughout this book as a figure 8 pattern. The horizontal figure 8 requires that a movement be performed on one side of the body followed by the other side of the body. We can also stimulate our brain by using our less dominant side to perform new skills. In rhythmic gymnastics, students are encouraged to use both hands and perform movements on both sides of their bodies and, thus, develop muscle control and coordination on the nondominant side.

Aesthetics

Rhythmic gymnastics is known as an artistic sport. Participants learn to use their bodies and the apparatus as tools of self-expression to communicate a theme, idea, or story. Rhythmic sequences that flow from one movement to the next communicate an aesthetic, visual story that pleases the eye of the viewer and the minds and bodies of the performers. In a rhythmic gymnastics unit, students at all levels are encouraged to create routines that revolve around a theme or evolve from a concept. (This is addressed further in chapter 4.)

Active Lifestyle

For many participants the sport of rhythmic gymnastics becomes a lifelong leisure activity. Gentle movement patterns are particularly suitable to people in the third stage of life, in the age 55 and older category. In European countries, males and females of all ages, abilities, and body types enjoy participating in rhythmic gymnastics and other types of gymnastics. One of my favorite performances at the 1999 World Gymnaestrada in Göteborg, Sweden, was a group of men who performed a rhythmic routine with small batons and colored disks. They were true showmen who had the audience clapping along to their rhythmic performance.

Gender and Individuality Issues

In the competitive realm, rhythmic gymnastics has traditionally been a sport for women. But in Japan, rhythmic gymnastics has emerged as a competitive sport for men. The men compete using rings (basically small hoops), clubs, ropes, and sticks. These routines are dynamic, precisely executed, and exciting to watch. It is important that educators do not fall prey to gender stereotypes. Teachers play a significant role in how children learn to accept or reject ideas. Thus, teachers can turn gender into a nonissue simply by appreciating that children are individuals, each with their own talents and interests, and involving boys in the sport of rhythmic gymnastics. In my own rhythmic gymnastics classes I have had girls who did not particularly enjoy the rhythmic program; I have also had boys who were innovative, excited, and enthusiastic about the sport.

Individuality also comes into play in the teaching of rhythmic gymnastics. A shy or otherwise reluctant student (boy or girl) may not want to perform a routine with scarves but may find challenge in skipping or performing rope and ball tricks. As mentioned earlier, the addition of an apparatus often transforms hesitant students into active participants who create movements and sequences freely and confidently. These students focus on their equipment and, thus, become less self-conscious and freer in their movement.

With so many choices in rhythmic gymnastics, the needs of each student can be met with a little flexibility and a little ingenuity. In other words, something will appeal to everyone. Above all, it is important to present the sport of rhythmic gymnastics with enthusiasm and excitement. Indeed, a positive approach to introducing rhythmic gymnastics will ensure the program's success.

Gymnastics for All and for Life

Rhythmic gymnastics is now widely recognized as a sport that is beneficial to all ages, from preschoolers to senior citizens who wish to stay active and social. Young children relish the opportunity to explore with a ribbon and watch its playful patterns. Elementary students like to challenge themselves with ball skills or skipping tricks. Middle school students refine these and other skills further, combining interesting elements to create sequences and routines.

The diversity in age among rhythmic gymnastics enthusiasts is exemplified at the World Gymnaestrada:

- The Dynamos, a group of senior citizens from Edmonton, Alberta, Canada, that performs captivating rhythmic and gymnastics routines, comprises men and women aged 55 to 74. These seniors, along with Special Olympians, performed together at the 1999 World Gymnaestrada in Göteborg, Sweden, and regularly amaze audiences around the country.
- The official U.S. delegation to the World Gymnaestrada in 1999 included participants from the age of 5 up to age 74.
- The Australian team, which of all delegates traveled the greatest distance to the 1999 World Gymnaestrada, comprises participants aged 7 to over 60.

Europeans have long realized the value of participation in gymnastics throughout their life span from childhood to their senior years for maintaining health and wellness. Their lifelong involvement in gymnastics in likely influenced by their early experiences in the sport and the high societal regard for gymnastics as a method of maintaining fitness and flexibility. North Americans have far to go in their understanding and appreciation of the long-term benefits of rhythmic gymnastics. The flowing and gentle movements of rhythmic gymnastics make it an ideal sport for all ages, but particularly for seniors, who do best with low-impact and gentle movement. By establishing a good rhythmic gymnastics foundation early in life, educators will be encouraging lifelong participation in the sport.

Safety

Safety is a primary concern for any educator in charge of ensuring the well-being of children. Along with physical activity comes a certain element of risk. Thus, it is the job—not to mention professional obligation—of teachers to minimize any such risk. Fortunately, rhythmic gymnastics is a safe gymnastics discipline. Rhythmic gymnastics does not involve inverted flight or launching from heights. Nevertheless, instructors must always be prepared, using the appropriate equipment and tools to minimize hazards and continually monitoring the program for potential risks.

Planning a Safe Program

Common sense would suggest that the school and teacher have a class list that includes student names, parent or guardian contact names, and pertinent medical information about each student. Teachers will want to have immediate access to a telephone and a first aid kit in case of an emergency. If untrained in first aid, teachers will need to know who has the proper training and qualifications on site. That said, anyone working with children on a regular basis should consider first aid or sport medicine training.

Within a rhythmic gymnastics unit, student safety can be assured through proper

- teacher preparation and training,
- use of progressions,
- selection of age-appropriate skills and activities,
- supervision and observation of participants, and
- arrangement and selection of equipment.

Basic Rhythmic Gymnastics Rules

Rhythmic gymnastics is a safe sport in general. Nevertheless, a few basic rules can help to ensure the safety of all participants. The following rules should be explained to students and then enforced by instructors.

- Use your own spatial and be aware of people around you.
- Wear gymnastics slippers or runners, or have bare feet to avoid slipping.
- Keep long hair tied back and remove loose or large hair accessories.
- Remove jewelry.
- Wear suitable gym clothing without zippers, buckles, or belts.
- Keep extra clothing, gym bags, shoes, and equipment away from the main activity area to avoid tripping accidents.

- When using a ribbon, be sure to grasp the end of the stick to avoid poking yourself or others.
- Apparatus, especially scarves and ribbons, can be slippery. Do not stand on them.
- Do not kick a rhythmic gymnastics ball. Doing so could injure your foot or damage the ball.
- Do not use rhythmic gymnastics clubs. These are difficult to master and are inappropriate for young children.
- Check hoops for sharp edges or protruding staples at the joint.

Summary

The benefits of rhythmic gymnastics are all-encompassing and include physical benefits and opportunities for social interaction and self-esteem building. Many of the skills developed within a rhythmic gymnastics program, such as hand-eye coordination and spatial awareness, transfer well to other sports. These basic skills are considered the foundation of a well-designed physical education program.

Rhythmic gymnastics is a safe form of gymnastics, making it highly suitable for all ages, populations, ability levels, and body types. Teachers do not need specific technical training to conduct a rhythmic gymnastics program, only an understanding of basic safety practices.

Now that you understand the background of the sport, it is time to get started on your own rhythmic gymnastics program. The next chapter discusses equipment. As you proceed through it and the rest of this book, enjoy the fun and learning along the way. The sport of rhythmic gymnastics can be a joy to teach and a pleasure to learn. Enjoy sharing your newfound knowledge with children as you begin teaching rhythmic gymnastics.

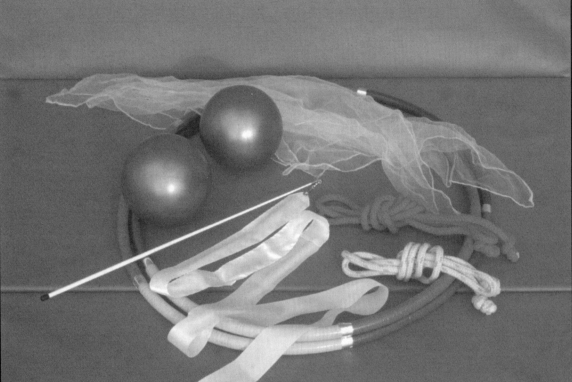

Rhythmic Gymnastics Equipment

Much of the equipment needed for a rhythmic gymnastics program may already be available in your school's physical education storage room. You can also purchase equipment from educational supply companies or, to save money, you can make your own equipment using readily available materials. The basic apparatus used in rhythmic gymnastics are ropes, hoops, balls, and ribbons. Scarves are considered alternative apparatus in rhythmic gymnastics. As noted earlier, clubs are not recommended for school- or community-based rhythmic gymnastics programs.

This chapter provides specific information on equipment, including construction steps to make your own as well as the proper care and maintenance of rhythmic gymnastics equipment.

Apparatus

The most familiar apparatus used in rhythmic gymnastics is the ribbon. Other basic hand apparatus include ropes, hoops, balls, and scarves (figure 2.1). Rhythmic clubs are used in competitive rhythmic gymnastics, but for safety reasons these are not recommended for school or community programs.

Alternative equipment choices may include small flags, rhythm sticks, tambourines, beach balls, or any other aesthetic piece of equipment that can be used in fun and novel ways.

Equipment Inventory Check

If you are just beginning to develop a rhythmic gymnastics program, availability of equipment may dictate its scope. Fortunately, there is enough equipment in most physical education storage rooms to begin a program. For a class of 30 students, for example, you could begin a rhythmic gymnastics program with 10 hoops, 10 ropes, and 10 suitable balls. You would simply set up three apparatus stations and have the students rotate to each apparatus station within a gym period.

If your school lacks even these basic physical education supplies, building up a rhythmic gymnastics equipment inventory can take awhile. In this case, the purchase of rhythmic gymnastics balls may be your soundest investment. Working with these well-balanced and weighted balls helps students feel the rhythmic qualities of balls. The purchase of hoops and ropes can also be easily justified in your program because they have many uses, both in the sport of rhythmic gymnastics as well as other physical education activities.

Before you make your shopping list for new rhythmic gymnastics equipment, see figure 2.2 for an example of an equipment inventory sheet. Once you know what you have on hand, you will know what you need. Then, you can

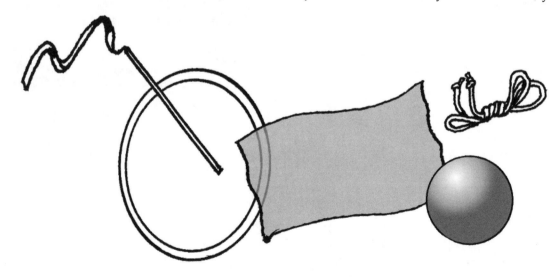

Figure 2.1 Rhythmic gymnastics apparatus for school programs: rope, hoop, ball, ribbon, and scarf.

Equipment	On hand	Condition	Quantity needed	To be purchased
Ropes: Plastic Braided				
Hoops: Small Large				
Balls: Junior Senior				
Ribbons: 5 meters Under 5 meters				
Scarves (small)				
Scarves (large)				

Condition of equipment: G = Good; F = Fair; P = Poor; R = Replacement needed.
From *Teaching Gymnastics: A Developmentally Appropriate Approach* by Heather C. Palmer, 2003, Champaign, IL: Human Kinetics.

Figure 2.2   Rhythmic gymnastics equipment inventory.

decide which equipment to purchase and which equipment you, parents, or other school volunteers can make.

For example, ribbons, which are unique to rhythmic gymnastics, can be made easily and inexpensively with some simple sewing. Employ the help of parents and school or community volunteers as well. With a little ingenuity, and a little time and effort, you can make these apparatus. Your students will love you for it, and you will gain so much personal satisfaction when you see a student try a ribbon for the first time.

Rhythmic Balls

One of the best choices for new rhythmic gymnastics equipment is a set of rhythmic balls. Rubber, plastic, or soft volleyballs or utility balls may be used, but rhythmic balls are better for a school program. Rhythmic balls roll smoothly and are weighted evenly. They are made of thick rubber and come in interesting colors. They can also come with lots of designs (e.g., metallic), which can be exciting to watch during a performance. When selecting a color, stay away from white or yellow because they soil easily. Also, choose a color that will appeal to both genders. I usually buy only two colors because it simplifies the distribution and collection of the equipment.

Rhythmic balls come in two sizes. The small size is the junior ball and measures 14 to 17 centimeters in diameter. Children aged 10 and under will experience greater success and mastery when using the junior ball. The large size is the senior ball and measures 18 to 20 centimeters. A suitable size and weight for older students and adults, the senior ball is the most widely available. Thus, if you need a junior ball, be sure to measure the ball before purchasing it.

Ball Care and Management

Rhythmic balls will last a long time if they are properly and carefully maintained. When inflating the balls, make sure that the tip on the pump is the right size. Also, be sure to lubricate the valve with liquid glycerin or soap before inserting it to preserve the life of the valve. Be sure not to overinflate rhythmic balls because doing so tends to distort their shape. Wash the balls occasionally with mild soap and water to maintain their shiny appearance, which is one of the things that makes them so appealing to play with. Store the balls in a cloth or canvas bag with a drawstring closure to help keep them clean. A hockey equipment bag is large enough to store a set of junior balls.

Ropes

The rope used for rhythmic gymnastics should be a braided synthetic rope approximately 1 centimeter thick. Many schools have plastic ropes with handles. These ropes are fine for speed skipping but are not suitable for rhythmic gymnastics. Soft braided ropes allow the students to perform rope skills, such as wrapping, more easily. To get the correct size, have students stand with both feet on the middle of the rope. The rope is the correct size when the

Figure 2.3 Sizing a rope.

ends of the rope reach shoulder level (figure 2.3). Knots can be tied on the ends of the rope to make them easier to catch and to prevent unraveling.

Make Your Own Ropes

To make your own ropes visit a hardware store that sells high-quality braided rope by the yard, foot, or meter. Choose a soft, pliable rope approximately 1 centimeter in diameter. Make sure the rope is braided, not twisted. In other words, do not use stiff, twisted nylon ropes that you might find in nautical supply stores. Because these ropes are not malleable, they are unsuitable for the sport. Rhythmic gymnastics ropes should be soft enough to wrap yet stiff enough to hold a nice shape during swings.

Cut the rope into the desired lengths and sear the ends of the rope to prevent unraveling. Wrap the ends of the rope with colored tape to further prevent fraying and to cover any rough spots produced during searing. Use different-colored tape for different rope lengths so that students will be able to choose their correct rope length easily and quickly. (Some supply companies sell colored rope in bulk, usually in 100-foot lengths and in up to four different colors. If you purchase these ropes, simply cut them to your desired specifications and sear the ends to prevent unraveling.)

Rope Care and Management

Ropes can be stored in a plastic tub or gym bag, grouped by color or size. Storage pegs, labeled by size or color, are also useful for rope storage. Before storing the ropes, have students fold the ropes into quarters and then tie them with a single overhand knot. Lead students through this procedure by having them complete the following steps (figure 2.4).

1. Fold the rope in half.
2. Fold the rope a second time so that it is quartered.
3. Step on the middle of the folded rope.
4. Tie a single overhand knot over the foot. (They take their foot out just before they tighten the knot.)

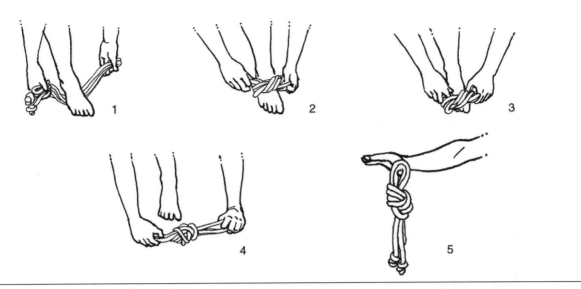

Figure 2.4   Tying a rope for storage.

Hoops

Many school equipment rooms are stocked with hula hoops. More often than not, however, these hoops are broken, bent, or misshapen. Nobody likes to play with a warped hoop. And the rough edges or staple joints on these broken or bent hoops can pose a safety risk. In the long run it is wise to invest in sturdy hoops. The sturdier the hoop, the longer it will last because it will not warp or bend easily. Although sturdy hoops are slightly more expensive, hoops are so very versatile—both in rhythmic gymnastics and other activities—that they are well worth the investment.

To make sure you have the proper hoop sizes on hand, have students stand next to the hoop and hold it on edge. The hoop should be no higher than the student's hip joint. Younger students will see the most success with a hoop 70 centimeters or smaller in diameter; older students will need a large hoop measuring 70 to 90 centimeters in diameter.

Make Your Own Hoops

It is even possible to make your own hoops. In some respects, homemade hoops are softer than the hoops you'll find at physical education equipment supply stores. The softer the hoop, the safer and easier it is to catch. Plus, if and when the hoops get bent or kinked, softer hoops are more easily repaired, simply by pushing out the bend or kink.

Hardware and home improvement stores, typically those with a plumbing department, often carry tubing that is appropriate for constructing hoops. The tubing comes in a bulk coil that can be cut into specific lengths and joined together to create durable hoops. Select tubing that is between 1.5 and 2 centimeters in diameter. For a 70 cm diameter hoop you will need a length of tubing that is 220 cm long. For a large 90 cm hoop cut the tube to a length of 282 cm. The tubing is easy to cut using a sharp knife or a small saw. Some hardware stores will cut the tubing for you in their store.

Hardware and home improvement stores will also sell joiners (or couplings) that will connect the two ends of the tube to make the circular shape. Simple insert the coupling into the open ends of the tubing and push together (figure 2.5).

Once you have your hoops assembled, make them more vibrant and eye appealing with colorful electrical tape. (Most tubing is black and unappealing.) Wrap the tape around the entire hoop, overlapping the edge of the tape as you work your way around the hoop. This tape also makes the hoops sturdier. For easy size identification, you may want to use different-colored tape for different hoop sizes.

Figure 2.5 Hoop construction: insert the coupling into the ends of the tubing to connect.

Hoop Care and Management

To prevent breaking or bending, hoops should not be pulled or squashed. Hoop storage is always a challenge. The best storage solution is to have large storage pegs on which to hang the hoops according to size.

You can also store hoops in their own covers. You can fit 9 to 10 hoops inside one cover. Adjust the elastic so that the hoops are held snugly but can be easily removed. Construct a hoop cover by completing the following steps (figure 2.6).

1. Select a piece of strong fabric (e.g., light denim, canvas) that measures 60 centimeters. Cut the length so that it is as long as the circumference of the hoop, plus 4 centimeters.

2. Sew the cut ends of the long fabric strip together to make a fabric loop.

3. Along the two edges of the fabric loop, fold over and sew 3 centimeters of fabric to make casings.

4. Thread strong elastic through the casings on each side and tie the ends together in a temporary knot. At this point, you should have something that resembles a large steering wheel cover.

5. Insert the hoops into the case and adjust the elastic tension so that the hoop cover can be easily removed.

Ribbons and Ribbon Sticks

Ribbon sticks may be made of plastic, fiberglass, or wood dowels. A swivel mechanism at one end of the stick allows the ribbon to twirl and spiral without becoming tangled. Ribbon sticks and ribbons can be purchased as sets, or you can buy them individually from rhythmic gymnastics supply companies or physical education supply catalogs. Commercially purchased ribbon sets come with the stick, ribbon, and the necessary hook and swivel attachment.

For competitive gymnasts, ribbon length is 5 or 6 meters. For schoolchildren, a shorter ribbon is easier to handle, although you want to be sure that the ribbon is long enough to maintain shape and form when moved through the air. Ribbons that are too short do not define the shape of the movement effectively.

Make Your Own Ribbons and Ribbon Sticks

For students over the age of 10, it is best to buy commercially produced rhythmic gymnastics sticks and ribbons. The flexible nature of a fiberglass stick and a longer ribbon length (5 meters) will better enable these students to manipulate the ribbon in exact ways and, hence, gain the most from their experience with ribbons. Working with an authentic piece of equipment is also more satisfying for older students. However, ribbons over 5 meters long are difficult to handle and may lead to frustration. In this case, it may be better to make your own ribbons and ribbon sticks.

Ribbon sticks are easy to make. To construct a stick, complete the following steps.

1. Purchase a wooden dowel (made from any type of hardwood) 1 centimeter in diameter.

2. Cut the dowel into 40 to 50 centimeter lengths (40 centimeters for children aged 5 to 7, 45 to 50 centimeters for older children aged 8 to 10). Sand the dowel shaft and ends thoroughly to eliminate rough spots.

3. At one end of the dowel make a grip using tape. Wrap the dowel from the end up to approximately 12 centimeters.

4. Insert an eye screw at the other end (unwrapped) of the dowel. Add a small split ring to the eye screw and then add a swivel hook to the split ring. Swivel hooks can be found in the fishing tackle department of most sporting goods stores. The swivel hook opens much like a safety pin and holds the end of the ribbon onto the stick.

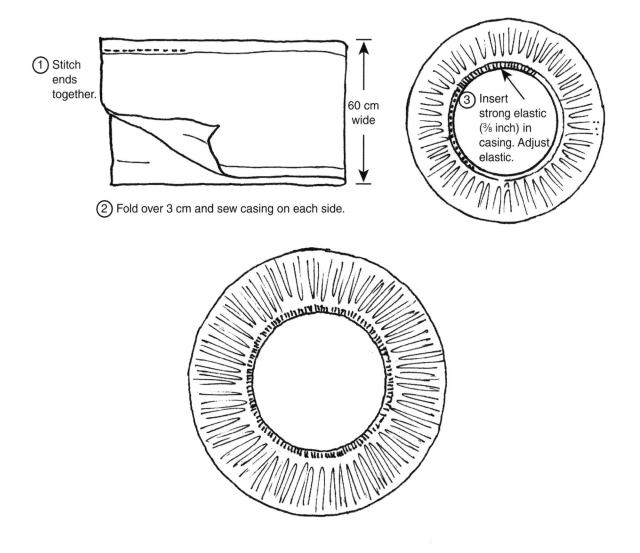

① Stitch ends together.

60 cm wide

③ Insert strong elastic (⅜ inch) in casing. Adjust elastic.

② Fold over 3 cm and sew casing on each side.

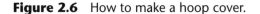

Figure 2.6   How to make a hoop cover.

If you can sew a straight seam, you can make your own ribbons, as outlined in the following steps (figure 2.7). At fabric supply stores you can often find ribbon sold by the yard or meter. Choose a satin ribbon that is made of nylon, viscose, or polyester and has a light feel to it. Do not choose acetate; it will fray too quickly and may have a sharp edge. Try to find ribbon that is 5 centimeters wide (this is the size of commercially produced ribbons).

1. Decide on the finished length of your ribbon and add 1 meter. For younger students the finished ribbon length should be between 3.5 and 4 meters; for older students, between 4 and 5 meters. Cut the ribbon to the appropriate length.

2. Fold the ribbon, wrong sides together, at the 1-meter mark and stitch the ribbon to itself (as close to the edge as possible). This double layered section adds stability to the ribbon.

3. At the fold, create a point by folding and matching the edges. Stitch this point into place. This point is where the swivel hook will be inserted to attach the ribbon to the stick.

4. Sew a small hem at the opposite tail end of the ribbon to prevent fraying.

Ribbon Care and Management

Ribbons can be the most exciting and visually appealing apparatus used in rhythmic gymnastics,

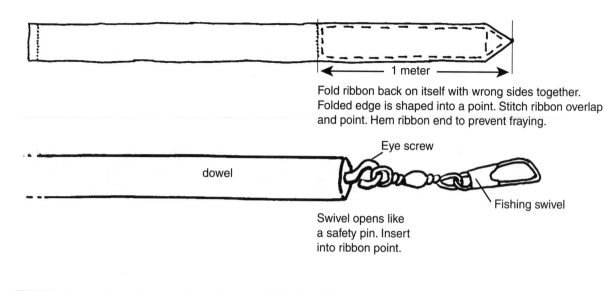

Figure 2.7 Ribbon construction.

but they also require the greatest amount of care and maintenance. Tangles, for example, are common. If not unraveled early, small tangles can quickly become knots that are too tight for anyone to loosen or untie. When it comes to ribbon care, the best precaution is prevention. When using ribbons in your class, frequently stop the group and ask for a knot check. If caught early, tangles and loose knots can be easily untangled.

Good ribbon technique will also help to minimize ribbon knots. Instruct students to keep the ribbon stick pointing down, toward the ground, when performing beginning skills such as circles, spirals, and snakes. In large movements, such as circles or figure 8s, students should use their greatest range of motion. When students use a smaller range of motion and, thus, speed up the ribbon movements, tangles occur. Simply remind students to slow down their manipulation and to let the ribbon flow.

Careful storage and care of ribbons and sticks will increase their longevity. Many ribbon tangles occur in the storage room when ribbons are moved or shifted to get at other equipment. If ribbons are already tangled or knotted when put away, the knots can tighten. Alleviate this problem by making a rule that ribbons must never be put away with a knot. For ribbons with wooden sticks, the best way to store them is to gently wrap the ribbon around the ribbon

stick and secure it with an elastic band. If the sticks are fiberglass, however, wrapping them in this manner may create holes in the ribbon.

When the ribbons become soiled, wash them by hand using water and a mild soap. Hang them to dry. Gently iron the ribbons while they're slightly damp on a low heat setting to straighten them. Never wash them in a washing machine or dry them in a dryer. If you do, you will be untying knots from now until next year!

Make Your Own Ribbon Storage System

A good solution to the ribbon storage problem is the use of carrying cases (figure 2.8). (Note: This carrying case works best for homemade ribbons with wooden sticks.) As with the hoops, you can make different cases for different-sized ribbons and ribbon sticks. Such a carrying case will also help keep them organized. Make your carrying cases by completing the following steps.

1. Choose a length of fabric that is twice as long as your ribbon stick length and about 1 meter wide.

2. Finish the edges of the fabric so that they will not fray by sewing with an overlock serger or by sewing with a wide zigzag stitch.

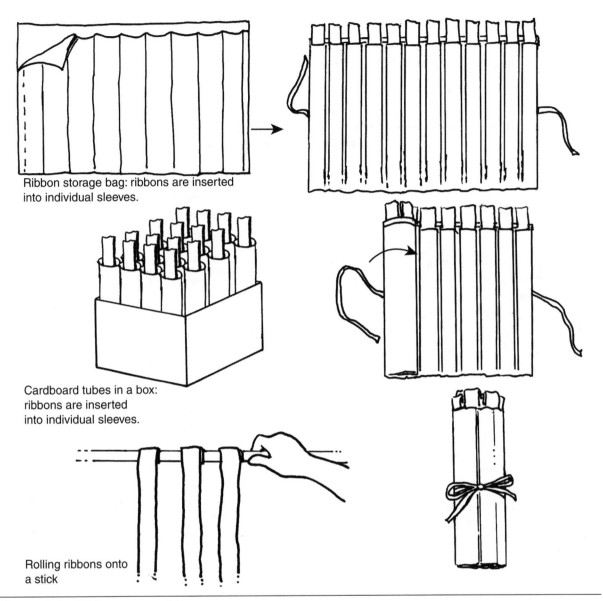

Ribbon storage bag: ribbons are inserted into individual sleeves.

Cardboard tubes in a box: ribbons are inserted into individual sleeves.

Rolling ribbons onto a stick

Figure 2.8 Ribbon storage ideas.

3. Create pockets for individual ribbon and stick sets by folding the material lengthwise and then sewing channels slightly larger that the width of the ribbon.

Then simply insert one ribbon and stick set into each channel. Once the ribbons are inserted, roll the carrying case (like a sleeping bag) and secure it with a tie to prevent it from unrolling.

An alternative and quick storage solution is to collect several cardboard tubes and cut them slightly shorter than the length of the ribbon stick. Stand the cardboard tubes upright in a box. Wrap each ribbon around its stick and insert into a cardboard tube to keep it tangle free.

For ribbons with fiberglass or plastic sticks, remove each ribbon from the stick and wind it into a roll. Store the rolled ribbons in a bag and store the sticks in a piece of cardboard tubing with one end sealed closed with tape. Special Olympics coach Meg Smale designed the following ribbon roller for her athletes.

1. Screw 5 or 6 small hooks along a piece of hollow tubing (dowels can also be used).

2. Remove the ribbons and swivel attachment from their sticks and hang them on the hooks on the tubing.

3. Twist or roll the tube so that the ribbons wind around it. Have a second person nearby to straighten the ribbons as they wind onto the tube.

If you use hollow tubing, this ribbon roller can also become a storage case for the ribbon sticks. Simply purchase two caps that fit the ends of the tube.

Scarves

Like ribbons, scarves are an exciting, attractive rhythmic gymnastics apparatus and are popular with all ages. The scarf's soft flowing movement translates into fluid and graceful routines. Scarves also have a calming effect when used in rhythmic gymnastics. This "silent" apparatus lends itself to more relaxed and softer movements. Purchase or make scarves using vibrant and bright colors as they will lend themselves well to large group performances where large bursts of color are needed.

Scarves are fun to use and, when mastered, easy to control. They often come in several bright colors and can be purchased from equipment supply companies and catalogs. (Scarves are sometimes listed in catalogs' juggling or creative movement equipment categories.) Young students typically use one or two small scarves. These are handheld and measure 50 by 50 centimeters. Older students typically enjoy small scarves as well as large scarves, which measure 1 meter by 2 meters.

Make Your Own Scarves

Scarves can also be homemade. All you need do is visit your local fabric store and purchase some light, transparent fabric. (Note: for juggling activities it is important to have 2 to 3 different colors of handheld scarves. Be sure to choose vibrant colors that will appeal to everyone.) Once you have your material, simply cut it to the desired length and width, then hem it using a serger (overlock sewing machine). To avoid having to hem the material after cutting it, find a fabric that does not fray.

Scarf Care and Management

Scarves of any size should be folded and stored in a breathable fabric bag or a carton that will allow air circulation. Another option for scarf storage is to gather them together at one corner and bind them with an elastic band. Then simply hang the elastic band on a storage peg or other hook in the equipment room. Once in a while, scarves can be washed. Use the washing machine's gentle cycle and dry them in the dryer using fabric softener sheets to reduce static.

Alternative Apparatus

When funds are limited, or even in addition to the traditional apparatus, consider using what are known as alternative apparatus in your rhythmic gymnastics program. This equipment can be made with a little effort and a little creativity. Look around you, in the school, at home, and around your community, to see what kinds of materials you have available—and don't skip the trash can. One ingenious teacher took all his broken hoops and cut them into half hoops. His students loved skipping with them and ended up creating some interesting movement sculptures using these alternative apparatus. Another instructor created tube routines using cardboard tubes discarded from a fabric store. Also consider modifying the equipment you have. One creative alternative apparatus, which was well received by students, was a scarf attached to the end of a ribbon stick.

Employ the minds of your students in coming up with alternative apparatus, too. Encourage them to brainstorm ideas for equipment and then create routines and movements using that equipment. One student, for example, created his own apparatus by attaching three scarves around the perimeter of a hoop. The visual effect of this rolling hoop was amazing; it looked like flickering flames during his routine.

The basic rule for creating alternative apparatus is that each apparatus should be visually appealing and safe to use. Beyond that, anything goes. Let your imagination lead the way. Here are a few suggestions for "alternative" equipment you might find in your supply closet or somewhere around school (figure 2.9).

- Beach balls
- Small flags
- Wide ribbons
- Plastic throwing disks and rings
- Large balloons
- Tambourines (commercial and home-made)
- Lummi sticks (i.e., rhythm sticks)
- Long sticks or tubes
- Maracas
- Parachutes

- Exercise bands or tubes
- Large exercise balls
- Half hoops
- Homemade percussion instruments (e.g., shakers, drums)

Facility

For a successful rhythmic gymnastics program, the facility must meet certain requirements. (A gymnasium or large dance studio is best.) Ceilings must be high enough so that thrown balls and hoops will not interfere with lights or other ceiling fixtures. The facility must be large, es-

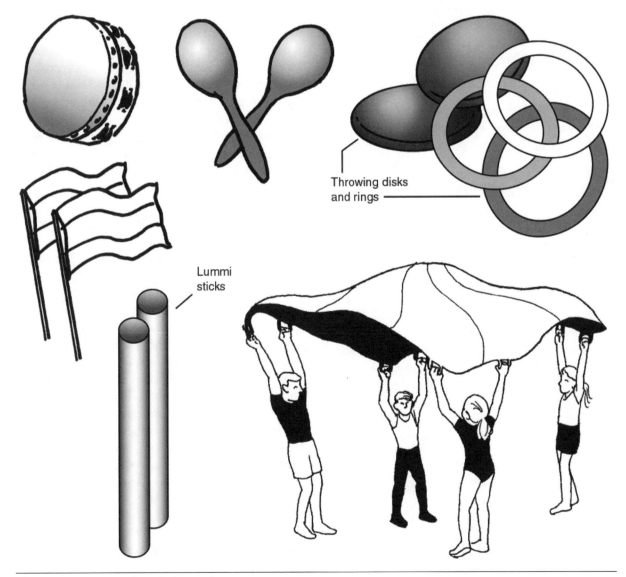

Throwing disks and rings

Lummi sticks

Figure 2.9 Examples of alternative apparatus.

pecially if you will be using ribbons. Students must have enough space so that their ribbons can move freely without becoming tangled with others' ribbons. This is important, both for participants' enjoyment and for safety. If your space is too small or too restrictive for everyone to use ribbons, you might consider using a second apparatus during class and then simply have students trade equipment partway through the lesson. For safety reasons, the perimeter of the facility should be free of obstacles and potential hazards.

As mentioned earlier, dance studios lend themselves well to a rhythmic gymnastics program. Students can watch themselves in the mirrors as practice skills and perform routines. Rhythmic gymnastics can also be taught outdoors, with certain modifications and adjustments, although the surface or ground should be flat to prevent tripping injuries. For example, many of the hoop, ball, and rope activities could be completed on an outdoor court or playing area. Ribbon and scarf activities, however, are best left for indoors as any wind or breeze will make these flowing apparatus difficult to control.

Sound System

Music is an integral part of any rhythmic gymnastics program. Thus, access to a high-quality sound system is important, although not essential. In a perfect world we would all have the sound system of our dreams. Of course, budget restraints often dictate what is available, particularly if the rhythmic gymnastics unit will be taught in a gymnasium. (Having a good sound system available is yet another reason dance studios work so well in teaching a rhythmic gymnastics unit.)

If you have the budget to upgrade your sound system, the following features are ideal.

- Good sound quality
- Multitrack CD and dual tape player (for greater music selection and variety)
- Capability to tape from a CD (to allow you to compile several appropriate songs on one tape)
- Removable speakers (to project the sound into a large space)

- Remote control (this allows you to keep your focus and attention on your students without having to turn your back and search for a certain musical selection)

You will also want to ensure that your sound system is safe and secure. Portability is important if you want to use the system in more than one location, but large systems are more secure. They can be securely installed to prevent theft and protect your investment.

Summary

Certain rhythmic gymnastics equipment will be a sensible investment for your program and school. Rhythmic balls are the most expensive but may be your soundest investment. They last a long time when cared for properly and the skills learned on them are invaluable to the sport. Hoops are also fundamental to the sport, but these can be used for all sorts of other activities as well. Ropes are affordable, portable, and offer endless opportunities for fitness through skipping and other rhythmic gymnastics skills. Ribbons, the apparatus unique to rhythmic gymnastics, will likely be the most popular piece of equipment in your rhythmic gymnastics program.

If funds are tight, many rhythmic gymnastics apparatus can be constructed. With the help and support of your school, local community, and students' parents, you can assemble a comprehensive rhythmic gymnastics equipment inventory in no time! Whenever possible, involve the students and their parents in making equipment (e.g., hoop taping, color selection of ribbons). When children have a hand in making the equipment they use, they develop a greater sense of responsibility for the care and maintenance of that apparatus.

Whether purchased or homemade, rhythmic gymnastics equipment will be an investment worth caring for to ensure that future generations have the equipment they need. Students can be trained at any age to assist with the maintenance and management of equipment. With a few simple rules and storage techniques, your rhythmic gymnastics equipment should last a long time.

The Six Stages of a Rhythmic Gymnastics Unit

Planning a rhythmic gymnastics unit can be an easy process when you open your mind to the endless possibilities of the sport. In the school setting there are no set strategies or rules for progressing through a rhythmic gymnastics program, nor are there strict parameters for skill development. Guidelines are provided to assist you through the six-step process outlined; however, remember that they are simply guidelines, not hard and fast rules of instruction. Instead, the sport and your instruction should evolve with the ideas, creativity, and skill development of your students. You need only provide the opportunities for self-exploration that progress into skill development and then skill refinement.

The starting point for a rhythmic gymnastics unit and the rate at which you proceed through the unit will depend on your students' prior physical education learning experiences If this experience and knowledge base are unknown, give your students an opportunity for some free exploration. By observing their exploration, you will quickly gain insight into their prior movement experience and be readily able to assess their skill level. Then, it's simply a matter of progressing through the six stages, which are explained in this chapter. These stages are based on sound common sense, knowledge of good teaching, and the stages of child development:

Stage 1: Spatial awareness without apparatus

Stage 2: Exploration and discovery with apparatus

Stage 3: Fundamental movement identification

Stage 4: Learning extension with tasks and challenges

Stage 5: Sequence and routine development

Stage 6: Demonstration and evaluation

Stage 1: Spatial Awareness Without Apparatus

Spatial awareness is the understanding of how to move through open areas, including exploration of different directions, pathways, planes, and levels. The space in which a student is able to move freely is commonly known as general or common space. Spatial awareness also includes a sense of personal space, which is each student's area for work and movement. All students should be taught to respect and stay clear of others' personal working space.

The development of good spatial awareness is important for a young child's complete physical development and safety. Children need to practice moving safely through spaces and must have keen awareness to move without bumping or crashing into others. This involves anticipating the movements of others. As a kindergarten teacher for many years, I found that focusing extensively on spatial awareness early in the year, before we moved on to other activities, was time well spent. I would then revisit this concept throughout the year.

Spatial awareness is particularly crucial when children begin to use large apparatus, such as ribbons and hoops. When children add an apparatus to their movement, their personal space must expand to accommodate the new extension of their bodies: the equipment. Then, when children begin creating their rhythmic sequences and routines, the concepts of level, plane, direction, and pathway are added to the mix. (Chapter 8 reviews the concepts of spatial awareness before presenting these advanced concepts.) Following the introduction to these concepts are activities that will help students develop spatial awareness before embarking on apparatus exploration and skill development. (Also included in chapter 8 are the fundamental body movements important to rhythmic gymnastics: locomotion, balance, jumps and leaps, and pivots and turns.)

Stage 2: Exploration and Discovery With Apparatus

In the next stage of a rhythmic gymnastics program, apparatus are added. Children of all ages will enjoy the opportunity to explore the apparatus independently in a self-directed manner. For some students, the feel of a ribbon may be a new experience. They will need time and plenty of opportunity to practice and investigate what they can do with this new piece of equipment.

Now is the time to set the guidelines for exploration. Students must use the equipment in a responsible manner, for their own safety and for the safety of others. Exploration is an important developmental stage for children, but it should not become an unfocused free-for-all. Before beginning any activity, structure students' exploration by giving them some guidelines (and rules if appropriate). When using scarves, for example, encourage students to explore all the different ways a scarf can move, such as waving, floating, and circling. When using ribbons, have students focus on circles and levels. Be sure to remind them to respect others' personal space.

Music can be a wonderful source of inspiration at this stage. Have students listen carefully to the music and respond using their bodies and certain apparatus. For example, when introducing ball if you choose music with a definite and pronounced beat, the students will likely respond with rhythmic ball bouncing. If you choose softer music, they will respond with more gentle movements such as swinging and rolling. Chapter 7 describes how to choose music that is appropriate for the different apparatus and for different age levels of students.

When introducing each apparatus, move from the familiar to the unfamiliar. Most children have had prior experiences with balls and ropes, for example, so it is best begin with these and then move on to introduce hoops, ribbons, and scarves. However, students are often eager to try all of the apparatus. When first introducing a rhythmic gymnastics unit, I like to set up apparatus stations around the gym and let each student try all of the equipment for a few minutes within one class time. Once students have had a chance to try each apparatus, they are often more willing to focus on the lessons.

Stage 3: Fundamental Movement Identification

As students explore each apparatus, they will begin to discover the fundamental elements for each apparatus. Balls are a great starting point for this process because almost all children will be familiar with the actions they can perform with a ball (e.g., bouncing, throwing, catching, rolling, and so on). In rhythmic gymnastics these actions are the fundamental ball elements. Lead students through a guided discovery of every movement they can perform with a ball. Chart these discoveries on a wall chart or check them off as they are discussed on the routine-planning forms (figure 3.1). Then, when they move on to a less familiar apparatus, the movement identification process will be more familiar to, and thus easier for, your students.

Help students identify the names of each fundamental movement they are performing by using words that describe each movement. When you use the ribbon, for example, the shape the ribbon creates or how the ribbon moves describes a fundamental movement (e.g., circles, spirals). I will often use students to demonstrate each movement and then name the movement. Or, I help them discover the appropriate label. At the exploration stage, for example, a student may perform a spiraling action of the ribbon. Oftentimes children will aptly describe this movement as a tornado or a twister. I then provide them with the correct technical movement name: the spiral.

It is important to communicate about all sports using a common vocabulary and language. Figure 3.2 is a word search to reinforce the vocabulary relating to rhythmic gymnastics. A common language helps teachers and students share ideas clearly and to show understanding of new ideas and concepts. You may need to supply them with the appropriate vocabulary or simply guide them to discover it on their own; this process depends on the age of your students. Take, for example, a figure 8 pattern. To help them in this discovery process, you can supply the vocabulary for

Date: _____   Class: _____

Name: _____

Group members:

Apparatus: _____

Music: _____

List the skills you are going to use in your sequence/routine.

Beginning position (balance):

Skills:

1.

2.

3.

4.

Ending position (balance):

Figure 3.1   Student routine-planning form.

From *Teaching Rhythmic Gymnastics: A Developmentally Appropriate Approach* by Heather C. Palmer, 2003, Champaign, IL: Human Kinetics.

```
S  E  Q  U  E  N  C  E  K  T  Y  G  E  T  A
N  F  F  E  L  C  R  I  C  S  Y  P  I  K  S
T  U  R  B  K  O  G  H  W  M  W  A  L  K  M
N  R  A  O  U  L  A  T  N  O  Z  I  R  O  H
E  L  A  T  N  N  E  A  K  L  L  O  N  T  T
L  N  I  V  O  T  E  A  A  P  E  F  D  G  Y
N  N  A  B  E  S  A  T  P  A  V  F  F  T  H
E  O  B  L  T  L  T  L  O  T  E  R  C  E  R
J  I  I  R  P  I  B  M  O  H  L  A  I  M  O
R  E  A  T  G  N  U  R  H  W  Y  C  M  P  P
Y  D  T  A  C  S  P  I  R  A  L  S  H  O  E
A  C  S  A  I  E  H  B  L  Y  F  J  T  N  W
V  I  D  C  E  B  R  T  O  V  I  P  Y  R  A
S  N  A  K  E  R  W  I  T  A  E  B  H  U  V
K  X  J  U  M  P  C  D  D  O  X  Z  R  T  E
```

BALL	RHYTHMIC
BEAT	RIBBON
CIRCLE	ROPE
CREATE	ROUTINE
DIRECTION	RUN
FRONTAL	SAGITTAL
FUN	SCARF
GYMNAESTRADA	SEQUENCE
HOOP	SKIP
HORIZONTAL	SNAKE
JUMP	SPIRAL
LEAP	SWING
LEVEL	TEMPO
MUSIC	TRAVEL
PATHWAY	TURN
PIVOT	WALK
PLANE	WAVE
RHYTHM	_____

Figure 3.2 Word search using rhythmic gymnastics vocabulary.
From *Teaching Rhythmic Gymnastics: A Developmentally Appropriate Approach* by Heather C. Palmer, 2003, Champaign, IL: Human Kinetics.

the fundamental movement and ask students to demonstrate what they think that movement might look like: "How would you draw the number 8 with your ball?" In some instances, a direct-teaching lesson may be needed.

Figure 3.3 outlines the fundamental elements for each apparatus. As you can see, many of the apparatus have similar elements. For example, you can perform a swinging motion using a hoop, ball, rope, ribbon, and scarf. You may want to focus your lesson on elements that are common to several apparatus. (Chapter 4 provides an easy-to-follow lesson plan to help you plan or record class rhythmic gymnastics lessons.)

Stage 4: Learning Extension With Tasks and Challenges

To reinforce the skills discovered within stages 2 and 3, stage 4 challenges students with tasks and challenges to help them expand their learning. In chapter 9, suggested challenges and tasks are listed under each of the fundamental elements for each apparatus. Many of these tasks and challenges encourage group work and cooperation. After you present each task,

allow students time to respond and then practice their newly acquired skill. By offering open-ended challenges, you will elicit a variety of creative and interesting solutions. In fact, you may see as many different solutions as you have students!

Stage 5: Sequence and Routine Development

Once students have had ample opportunity to explore and develop skills within the different fundamental movement categories, they will be prepared to begin linking the skills they have learned into sequences or short routines. Skills from different movement categories are linked together in a smooth, flowing manner. A sequence is a chain of three to four skills linked together, usually with a beginning and an ending static position. A routine is longer and will include several sequences linked together. Younger children, ages 5 to 9, can create simple sequences that use a variety of movements. Students age 10 and older can create more intricate sequences that are then put together to make routines. Creating sequences or routines is a wonderful way for students to review what

Rope	Hoop	Ball	Ribbon	Scarf
Swing	Swing	Swing	Swing	Swing
Jump and skip	Circle	Circle	Circle	Circle
Rotate	Roll	Roll – body – floor	Spiral	Wave
Wrap	Spin	Figure 8	Figure 8	Figure 8
Throw and catch	Throw and catch	Throw and catch	Snake	Throw and catch
Release	Rotate	Bounce		
	Pass over or through			

Figure 3.3 Fundamental elements for each apparatus.

they have learned and weave it together into a demonstration. Many students will naturally want to share their sequences and routines with others, which can evolve into a great opportunity for peer mentoring and instruction.

For younger students, simply ask for a sequence that has beginning and ending positions with three skills in between. Using the ball, for example, these three skills might include a bounce, a roll, and a throw and catch. Using the ribbon, you might ask for a swing, a circle, and a spiral. For more advanced students, sequences can be much more intricate—focusing, for example, on using different spatial awareness themes (e.g., pathways, planes, levels, direction) or including fundamental body elements (e.g., pivots, jumps and leaps, locomotion, balances). Older students can also link sequences together to form long, elaborate routines.

Once students are ready to create sequences, there are several ways to proceed. You may want to specify open-ended routine requirements and allow students to create routines based on their own interests and desires. An open-ended routine requirement might be to tell them to create a routine using their choice of apparatus and show five different skills with a beginning and ending balance. (The student routine-planning form, figure 3.1, will help students organize and record the routine they create.) This form changes as they create and choreograph the routine and becomes a blueprint for the finished routine.

A second choice may be to use the routine-planning posters to outline the fundamental elements of each routine and then allow students to choose skills they want to include. To use the routine-planning posters in the appendix, copy or enlarge them to 11 by 17 inches on a copier. Then laminate and post them around the gym. Simply check off the apparatus elements (using erasable marker on the routine-planning posters) you would like to see combined in a routine. To offer them choice, you might create a routine plan for three apparatus and have students choose the apparatus they wish to use for their routine.

The routine plan can be as specific or as general as you wish. You might ask older students to show levels, planes, direction, or pathways in their routine. If so, simply check off the specific movement you would like to see demonstrated. Also included on the routine-planning posters are body movements (e.g., pivots, leaps and jumps) and space requirements. Be cautious about imposing too many requirements on each routine because students will likely become more concerned with following the routine plan than being creative and using their imaginations to create a routine.

Sequences and routines can be created by individuals or pairs, or in small groups of three to five students. Group work promotes teamwork and collaboration. It also allows you to observe leadership skills and abilities among students. Group work adds interesting group dynamics to the movements and creates more interesting routines. For example, one half of the group may perform a skill followed by the second half of the group. Or group members may perform a few connected skills followed by each individual member of the group performing a couple of solo skills. Another way to develop teamwork and cooperation is the exchange of apparatus partway through the routine or by having the group change their formation on the floor.

Chapter 10 explains in more depth how to assist students in routine planning, how to create further challenge in routine development, and how to refine rhythmic gymnastics movements. Suggestions for increasing the visual appeal of routines and preparing for a performance are also outlined in this chapter.

Stage 6: Demonstration and Evaluation

This is the final stage of a rhythmic gymnastics program. Once students have had the opportunity to practice their sequences and routines, they perform them in front of their classmates. Whether or not you proceed to this stage is your own choice, likely based on the age, skill level, and preference of your students.

Another factor in deciding whether or not to proceed to this stage of a rhythmic gymnastics program is how you want to evaluate students. Perhaps your emphasis will be on the learning that has occurred during class time, focusing on the process. Or perhaps you will want to take your students further along before introducing the demonstration and evaluation stage.

For older students, demonstration and evaluation provide an excellent opportunity to teach peer assessment and self-evaluation. Students who enjoy the performing aspect of this sport may want to perform their rhythmic routines to a larger audience at a special event or assembly. For these students you might consider videotaping the routines and showing them at student-led conferences or open houses. (Chapter 10 discusses the process of routine assessment and evaluation. Figure 10.3 provides you with a teacher assessment checklist to assist in the evaluation process.)

Summary

Planning a rhythmic gymnastics unit is a relatively simple process, and it can be fun. Where you start on the six-stage continuum presented in this chapter will depend on your students' prior learning experiences. As educators know, planning for instruction is a flexible process. It evolves as group dynamics unfold and as vibrant and eager students share their ideas and opinions. An open-ended approach to rhythmic gymnastics will enable you to meet the needs of each student in your class. If you help students express their ideas, encourage them to move their bodies in new and exciting ways, and build in successes along the way, you will be well on your way toward implementing an effective rhythmic gymnastics unit that will be rewarding for all.

Planning the Rhythmic Gymnastics Unit

The starting point for a rhythmic gymnastics unit will depend on the previous experience and age level of your students. Those with a good understanding of movement themes without apparatus will be able to progress to movement exploration with apparatus. Those who have been exposed to rhythmic gymnastics exploration in earlier grades will have the prior experience to move quickly into routine development and group activities.

This chapter will lead you through the process of planning a rhythmic gymnastics unit for your students. By reading this book you will develop a good sense about the sport (and how it differs from other gymnastics disciplines) and appreciate its importance as part of a physical education program. You will need to establish a starting point for your group of students based on their past movement experiences. Once you establish a starting point, you can begin planning the unit and how far along the continuum (as outlined in chapter 3) you hope to take your group of students.

What Do I Have to Know?

To teach rhythmic gymnastics you simply need to structure the learning environment by providing opportunities for safe exploration of the equipment. Help children identify the movements that are specific to the chosen apparatus and encourage them to expand their learning. You do not have to be an expert who knows and can demonstrate the skills to students. All you need do is set up a learning environment that will support the students as they discover what they can do with their bodies and as they learn how to manipulate the equipment in an integrated and connected way.

Trust your instincts as a teacher. More important, show your confidence in the children. They will rise to meet your expectations. Take a moment to reflect on your past experiences as an educator. You have so much to give your students from your prior experiences. Perhaps you have experience teaching educational gymnastics, or you have knowledge about creative dance and movement. Applying what you know about children and their growth and physical development to a rhythmic gymnastics unit will be your best guarantee of success. We know that children learn best when they are motivated intrinsically, when they feel confident in their abilities, and when they are actively involved in the learning. If rhythmic gymnastics is new to you, think of it as a great opportunity to learn—about the sport, about your students, and about yourself. Learning a brand new skill as an adult can also provide a good perspective of what it is like to be a student trying something new for the first time.

Where Do I Start?

You have already started by reading this book and familiarizing yourself with the sport of rhythmic gymnastics. By becoming informed and knowing the basics, you are well on your way to leading a successful rhythmic gymnastics unit. Remember, with the exception of safety and caring for the equipment, there are no set rules and regulations that govern the sport at this level. Instead, your and your students' creativity and your ability to facilitate a learning situation will steer your course. Enabling students to explore and discover physical movements on their own will foster their growth and development and will give them the self-confidence to become risk takers in life.

To plan rhythmic gymnastics lessons and instruction, your first task is to evaluate and assess the prior movement experiences of your students. If you do not know the prior experiences of your students, simply observe them in activity to see how able and knowledgeable they are about movement.

- Have they developed a sense of their personal spatial and general gym spatial?

- Do they understand that movements can be performed at different levels (i.e., high, medium, and low)?

- Have they demonstrated the ability to perform locomotion skills using different pathways (e.g., straight, curved, zigzag, random)?

- Do they have a sense of movement direction (e.g., forward, backward, sideways, diagonal)?

For their own personal well-being, students will need to demonstrate their ability to move through gym spatial safely and to find their own personal spatial within the gym. (If students need to work on spatial awareness, chapter 8 provides ideas for developing spatial awareness.) After establishing a good understanding of spatial awareness, you can proceed to the rhythmic gymnastics unit with the introduction of handheld apparatus in chapter 9.

Connections to Core Physical Education Curriculum

The length of time you devote to a rhythmic gymnastics unit will depend on school curriculum requirements, students' prior experience with rhythmic gymnastics, access to rhythmic gymnastics equipment, and the number of classes. Many physical education curricula emphasize movement education, fitness, dance, rhythmic activities, games, and gymnastics within the scope of the total physical education program. Rhythmic gymnastics brings many of these topics together in one unit.

Rhythmic gymnastics truly is an all-encompassing sport. Movement education concepts are covered under the umbrella of spatial awareness, the first phase of a rhythmic gymnastics unit. Visually, the sport sometimes looks effortless, but it involves many fitness components. For example, rhythmic gymnastics combines locomotion that involves the lower body with apparatus work that involves the upper body. Skipping skills are also excellent for developing overall fitness.

The dance component of most physical education curricula is of course included in rhythmic gymnastics activities, but rhythmic gymnastics goes further. Unlike most physical education dance units, which typically involve only a few basic steps students must perform again and again throughout a single dance, rhythmic gymnastics encourages students to delve into their creative potential. They get to explore movement using free skills (i.e., no hand apparatus) and skills with apparatus (e.g., scarves, ribbons), and they get to apply creativity in designing their own sequences and routines. Greater rhythmic awareness is also developed in this sport. In other physical education dance units, students perform the same dance steps to the rhythm of the music. In rhythmic gymnastics, students develop an appreciation for what their bodies can do with certain rhythms by learning to physically interpret and communicate those rhythms differently each time.

Games are an integral part of any physical education curriculum. They keep the learning environment fun, first of all, but they also foster team building, cooperation, and skill development. By incorporating warm-up games into each rhythmic gymnastics lesson, you can also satisfy these requirements. Use high-intensity tag games that encourage active participation from all students to increase heart rate and also to help develop spatial awareness.

Understanding the Term *Gymnastics*

The last component of physical education curricula, gymnastics, is rather broad. At the school level, *gymnastics* is an all-encompassing term that has come to include artistic gymnastics, acrobatic gymnastics, stunt gymnastics, and educational movement gymnastics. Understanding the different types of gymnastics will help you make an informed decision about what type of gymnastics is the best for your teaching situation and also help you determine what is developmentally appropriate for your students.

Artistic gymnastics is the style of gymnastics with which most people are familiar. This is the style most seen on television, particularly during the Olympics. Artistic gymnasts are required to perform technically specific skills on large equipment or mats. Schools are moving away from this type of gymnastics, however, to protect themselves from issues of liability. For teachers to instruct artistic gymnastics, they should have specific skills and training in order to ensure the safety of each participant.

Stunt gymnastics, also known as stuntnastics, sport-acro, and acrobatic gymnastics, or acrobatics, involves such activities as making pyramids and performing other group and partner skills. Stuntnastics usually involves tricks or stunts that involve partner work and incorporates elements of artistic gymnastics such as headstands, handstands, and rolls. Again, teachers should have specific training in this area to ensure the safety of students. Pyramid-building activities, in particular, should be avoided when teaching young students. Young children simply do not have the skeletal or muscle strength to bear the weight of another child of the same size and age.

Educational movement gymnastics encourages children to explore movement tasks using their own creativity and ideas. Students learn specific tasks or challenges and then learn to interpret these movements using their own ideas and interpretation.

Developmentally Appropriate Practice

As educators, we must question what we are doing in our gymnastics programs to ensure that we are delivering programs appropriate for the age and abilities of students. Rhythmic gymnastics incorporates a developmentally appropriate approach by allowing children to proceed at their own level.

In teaching rhythmic gymnastics, you must provide opportunities for individual practice, skills and movements students can work on at their own pace but simultaneously within the group. Individualized practice is especially important when students demonstrate great variance in skill and prior movement experiences. As teachers, your challenge will be to find ways to keep all students motivated and challenged individually while ensuring maximum participation and activity within a class period.

The good news is, the very nature of this sport will help you meet that challenge. Rhythmic gymnastics provides endless opportunities for individuals to create and innovate at their own level and pace. Once you teach the basic skills, students will have a good foundation for further developing their skills. They simply perform the skills they feel comfortable performing and then interpret the tasks and challenges presented to them in their own way. Rhythmic gymnastics encourages individual creativity and each child's ability to create interesting movements and sequences with or without equipment. What's more, the risks are minimal. A developmentally appropriate rhythmic gymnastics unit will ensure that all students experience success.

Planning the Unit

As explained earlier, the time you spend on a rhythmic gymnastics unit will be influenced by the prior experience of your students. If they have extensive experience in spatial awareness and movement concepts and if they have explored the use of the rhythmic gymnastics equipment in prior years, you can move your group quickly through a review and onto sequence and routine building.

My own school has been very supportive of a rhythmic gymnastics program, and teachers have bought into the idea. Therefore, by the time my third-grade students get to my class, they have already been exposed to the various apparatus and have already developed an idea of how to build simple sequences. My job is simply to teach them more complex and intricate skills, and to guide them in refining their movement. If your students do not have prior rhythmic gymnastics experience, you may want to allocate more time to establish a good foundation for future learning experiences.

The equipment you have available will influence how you introduce the different apparatus within a rhythmic gymnastics unit. If you have enough equipment for each student, the class can learn and practice each task and challenge as a group. Even in the case of minimal equipment, however, you can still operate a good program by setting up stations to introduce students to each apparatus; making your own equipment (at a fraction of the cost of purchasing new equipment); or using available equipment (e.g., substitute utility balls for rhythmic balls). (See chapter 2 for details.)

Your rhythmic gymnastics unit plan should also factor in scheduled school activities. For example, you may want to plan your rhythmic unit so that it ends prior to a special event such as a school open-house or celebration evening, thus giving your students an opportunity to showcase their routines. Unit planning has to remain flexible to accommodate the ever-changing schedules in schools and the dynamic nature of students (different groups will progress through the rhythmic unit at different rates).

Unit Organization

Physical education program organization and class time should also be considered. Ideally, a complete rhythmic gymnastics lesson can be taught in 30 minutes. Set-up time is brief, and if instructional time is kept to a minimum, students usually have ample time to achieve class goals (see chapter 5 for guidelines on lesson development).

It is best if the rhythmic gymnastics unit is consecutive, covered over 4 to 8 weeks. If there is too much time between lessons, students will have difficulty progressing, oftentimes having to review where they left off in the previous lesson. A large gap between lessons is especially difficult if students are in the process of creating their own sequences, although routine-planning posters (see appendix) can help them remember the specifics of their routines.

To maintain interest, you might consider varying the activities within the unit. For example, I sometimes alternate between open-ended creative activities (e.g., gymnastics and movement) and sport-specific activities such as floor hockey or organized games. This adds variety to my curriculum and satisfies the diverse learning interests of my students. Gauge your students' level of interest throughout the unit. Then modify your lesson plan to add more variety as needed.

In structuring the unit, I sometimes divide it according to apparatus, covering one piece of equipment over a weeklong activity plan. That way, if everything is not covered in one class time, it can be carried over and continued the next day. I typically allocate two weeks for the ball because there are so many skills involved (e.g., throwing, catching, bouncing, rolling, partner exchanges). I like to devote more time to the rope as well, usually an additional 2 weeks as I also combine other fitness activities (e.g., endurance skipping) when I teach rhythmic gymnastics rope skills.

You may prefer to structure the unit by specific elements common to each apparatus (see figure 3.3). Note the overlap among many apparatus. For example, you can perform a swinging element with the rope, hoop, ball, ribbon, and scarf. This type of unit structure works especially well when equipment is limited. Set up a circuit of apparatus stations. After learning the element for that class, students rotate to each equipment station and try that element using each apparatus. Students often enjoy this approach because they get to try more than one piece of equipment within a class period.

Planning for Student Diversity

Rhythmic gymnastics is an inclusive sport; it's for everyone. As introduced earlier, students' learning needs are diverse. In addition to age-related characteristics, including attention span among others, students have varying learning styles, different emotional needs, and distinct personalities and abilities. Students who have difficulty expressing themselves verbally, for example, often enjoy rhythmic gymnastics because it offers them a way to share their emotions and ideas with others.

With a few modifications to your rhythmic gymnastics unit, you can deliver a suitable, motivating, and individualized program that will accommodate every student. When designing an individualized program for a special needs student, for example, the first step is to familiarize yourself with that child's specific needs. Review school records, conduct a personal interview, and observe the student in an active setting. You will also want to inquire about the student's perceptions of physical education to assess self-confidence level. Once this assessment is complete, look for ways to modify the program. It may be something as simple as creating a smaller hoop, adding a taped handgrip to a ribbon stick, using a smaller ribbon, or adding a wrist strap to a scarf. Skills can be modified or simplified as well. For example, if the class is trying different bouncing pattern with a ball, a simplification of that skill would be to have a student lower and raise the ball in a pattern mimicking the bouncing action of a ball.

Assessment

Assessment of student progress is an ongoing process that involves not only the teacher and the student but also the student's peers. Educators are moving toward a more authentic, broad-based assessment in which students have say in evaluating their own learning. Such an assessment entails evaluating learning through observation and anecdotal records in an authentic manner rather than in artificial, contrived situations. Self- and peer assessment can be done through written responses, journal entries, surveys, questionnaires, and even simple conversations.

Program Assessment

To provide students with the best possible program, we educators are taking a critical look at our own practices. When we evaluate the effectiveness of a unit, we are really evaluating our own effectiveness. Evaluating and assessing student learning on an ongoing basis is part of our professional obligation, and part of our journey, as teachers. Daily assessment and evaluation of the learning allows us to make adjustments and modify our methods to benefit the learner.

The dynamic, ever-changing nature of children also necessitates frequent teacher self-evaluation. Children may respond to an open-ended, problem-solving approach in one area but require a more teacher-directed approach in another. The following key questions may help you determine your effectiveness at leading students to the desired learning outcomes:

- Were students active and engaged in the activities and the learning?

- Did the activities accommodate differences in skill level?
- Did the activities to appeal to *all* students, taking into account gender, diversity, and special needs?
- Was there an appropriate balance of instructional time and active participation?
- Was participation and involvement maximal?
- Did students demonstrate safe practices?
- Are students tapping into their creative potential?
- Did students feel supported and encouraged when attempting new skills?
- Was ample practice time allowed?
- Did the skills presented build on prior student knowledge?

By asking these questions, by continually questioning and improving your own personal growth and development as teachers, you will be better able to evaluate your daily lessons and, thus, foster student learning.

Peer Assessment

Peer assessment simply involves students evaluating students. Peer assessment, of course, should be approached with sensitivity and awareness of individualism and diversity. Guidelines for giving and receiving feedback should be reviewed before starting the peer-assessment process. In written form, peer assessment can provide anecdotal documentation for evaluating student learning.

Methods for peer assessment are numerous. Students can evaluate the ability of their own group to complete a task successfully, or they can evaluate classmates' finished routines or sequences. The group can establish other criteria or help design a set of rubrics so that everyone can have a voice in the evaluative process. These rubrics could include such things as the ability to work within the structure of the group, communication skills, and level of contribution.

The following questions can help your students generate the criteria by which they will evaluate themselves and their peers. The second set of questions will assist students with the evaluation of their routine as it relates to use of fundamental elements, music, and spatial awareness themes.

Questions about group work

Did our group cooperate?

Did everyone participate?

When we had a problem were we able to solve it?

Did everyone have the opportunity to contribute their ideas?

Were we able to complete the assigned task?

A sample of a student questionnaire regarding group work is provided in figure 4.1.

Questions about finished routines

Were our movements visually appealing?

Did we stay in time to the music?

Did we change formations? Change levels? Use different pathways?

Did we involve our entire bodies in the movement?

Did we show a variety of movements?

Did we show control of the apparatus?

Did we show a beginning and an ending balance?

Self-Assessment

In assessing themselves, students have the opportunity to reflect on what they've learned and to make sense of it in their own ways. Self-assessment can be undertaken outside of gym

---

Date: _____

Name: _____

Group members: _____

_____

1. How well did your group work together?

2. What was your favorite part about working with this group?

3. Did everyone have a chance to share ideas?

4. Did you have any problems along the way?

   If yes, how did you solve the problem?

5. With whom would you like to work again?

   Why?

From *Teaching Rhythmic Gymnastics: A Developmentally Appropriate Approach* by Heather C. Palmer, 2003, Champaign, IL: Human Kinetics.

Figure 4.1   Sample questionnaire for evaluating groups.

time and may take the form of a survey, a drawing, a journal entry, a letter to a friend, or a one-on-one conversation or interview. Whatever the form, students should reflect on what they have gained from the experience, how they feel about the experience, and what goals they would like to work toward in the future.

You may be asking yourself how in the world you'll find time for physical education assessment when you have so much to do in other subject areas. It's a good question, but the bottom line is that self-evaluation is crucial to any learning environment. By giving students a chance to communicate about their experiences, you gain the opportunity to know your students better and on another level. Also, when it takes place outside of the gym, assessment can be a means of connecting the importance of physical activity to overall health and well-being, a crucial educational topic common to many health curricula. Students gain from the assessment experience as they come to sense the importance of their own physical development and overall personal growth.

Methods of Assessment

There are many ways to assess student learning in a rhythmic gymnastics unit. The goal is to observe student growth and development as they proceed through the rhythmic gymnastics unit, but it is also helpful to observe how they pull together what they've learned into a sequence or routine. In other words, assess the learning process first, then the finished product.

The following list includes methods of assessment using peers, and teacher as the evaluator. The list also includes ideas for student self-evaluation.

Observation and anecdotal comments: The teacher observes students' skills and abilities during class time and records such things as effort, participation, skill development, and cooperation.

Individual skill demonstration: Individual students demonstrate a skill for the class. The skill can be self-evaluated or assessed by peers or by the teacher. This skill can also be taught to the entire group as peer teaching.

Individual routine demonstration: Individual students combine skills into a sequence or routine and perform them for their classmates and teacher. The routine can be self-evaluated by the demonstrating student, or by peers or by a teacher.

Small group routine presentations: Student groups perform a sequence or routine for their classmates and teachers. The routine is evaluated by the group members, by peers, or by the teacher.

Schoolwide performances: Large groups of students perform a routine for the entire student body as part of an assembly or special event.

Teacher checklists: The teacher maintains ongoing skill checklists for students and evaluates a sequence or routine based on set criteria.

Student checklists: Students record their own progress on each apparatus or skill. When they have completed a required number of tasks, they can proceed to another apparatus or a more advanced skill level.

Connecting to Classroom Learning

Rhythmic gymnastics activities can be connected to learning that occurs in the classroom. Rather than keep physical education lessons isolated, it is important to help students find the connections that make their lives more meaningful. Connecting gym activities to lessons and concepts being discussed in other classrooms can be tricky. But with a little creativity and imagination, it's certainly possible.

At my children's school, for example, the class had written a story about the rainforest and then turned it into a play. I attended the play and was delighted to see that they decided to illustrate the sun by spiraling red, orange, and yellow ribbons. Thunder and rain echoed on stage with the strong rhythmic bounce of balls. These rhythmic props were important to their storytelling and allowed the children to use their rhythmic gymnastics skills in a way that was meaningful to their story.

Early in my own teaching career, I worked with a music teacher to combine our choir and rhythmic gymnastics club activities into an assembly. When the choir sang, a group of students performed their interpretation of the choral piece using handheld white scarves. It was truly a visual and auditory treat. To apply their learning about the water cycle, class members created a flowing river using large blue scarves. This was accompanied by student poetry readings relating to water and river conservation. When working with a fourth-grade class, I was able to combine some science concepts into the rhythmic gymnastics unit. To expand on students' understanding of light and shadow, for example, we created rhythmic routines that used black lights to illuminate fluorescent apparatus.

Connecting rhythmic gymnastics activities to classroom learning gives students an opportunity to express themselves and their ideas in a physical and kinesthetic manner. As teachers, when we help children connect to the world with their minds and their bodies, we are in fact contributing to their total development.

Summary

An important advantage of rhythmic gymnastics is that it can satisfy all the components of a physical education program. The sport of rhythmic gymnastics combines elements from movement education, fitness, games, dance, rhythmic activities, and gymnastics.

Planning a rhythmic gymnastics unit for your students begins with familiarizing yourself with their prior movement experiences and spatial awareness. If students have a solid foundation in spatial awareness, proceed to working with apparatus; if not, it's best to start your program with basic spatial awareness and movement instruction. Once you have established a starting point for your group, the program plan simply becomes a structure for providing opportunities for exploration and skill development with apparatus. The program may require minor adjustments here and there, including some simple equipment modifications for certain students, but rhythmic gymnastics is a developmentally appropriate sport. Because it allows individuals to progress at their own pace and ability, it is safe, it is fun, and each child experiences personal success.

Assessment is important when teaching a rhythmic gymnastics unit. The types of assessment include self-assessment, peer assessment, and program assessment, which includes teacher self-assessment. The methods of assessment include observation, the use of checklists, performances, and demonstrations. Any of these assessment types and methods enables you to measure student progress on an ongoing basis and, if necessary, modify your teaching style or lessons as you progress through the unit.

Whenever possible, it is a good idea to connect rhythmic gymnastics activities to classroom learning. This provides students with yet another avenue for exploring their understanding of important ideas and concepts.

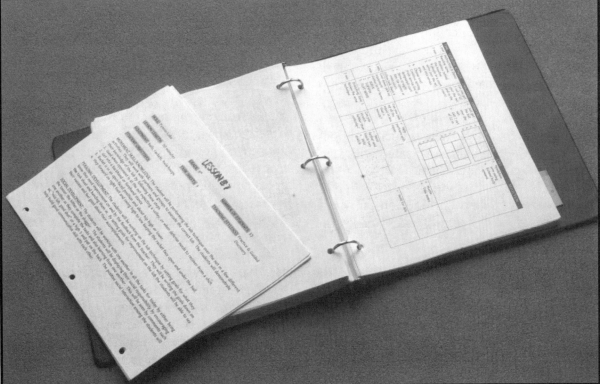

Developing the Lesson

Now that you have established a starting point for your group of students, you can begin developing the lessons that will constitute your master unit plan. The first step is to identify the learning outcomes you hope to achieve within a class period. Then it is simply a matter of selecting activities and learning challenges that will help students meet these objectives. The basic lesson-planning frame is outlined in this chapter as lesson introduction, body of the lesson, and closure. By remaining flexible in our planning, we are able to adapt to the ever-changing dynamics of a group of students as we find ourselves covering more in one lesson than planned. Or you may find that you wish to devote more time to an apparatus and revisit the skills associated with it in the next lesson. An important aspect of planning is evaluation. Was the lesson effective in leading students to the desired outcomes? Questions are provided to help you assess the lesson and plan for future student learning.

Learning Outcomes

Before you plan a lesson, ask yourself this simple question: "What learning outcomes would I like to see this group of students achieve during this lesson?" For younger students, your answer may be simply to have them experience new apparatus. For a more experienced group of students, a learning outcome might be to refine self-choreographed routines. You might also want to see how students work and cooperate in group activities, or perhaps you want your lesson to focus on the importance of health and safety in the sport. Figure 5.1 is a chart of possible learning outcomes divided into categories of safety, group work, skill development, attitude, and musicality. Or create your own learning outcomes that reflect the needs of your particular group of students.

Lesson Planning

Once you know where you want to go, begin a draft of how you plan to structure the lesson. I use the word *draft* to encourage you to write a lesson that will act as a guide or a reminder of where you would like to lead your group, not a scripted outline of a lesson. Even after many years of teaching, I find that I still need a plan to help me focus and stay on track, yet I want to remain flexible and open to the ideas and input of my students. Being the innately creative beings they are, students will bring their own ideas to the activities and tasks you put before them. From these ideas and the process of discovery you may find more innovative ideas and methods for proceeding.

When I follow the lead of my students, my lesson plan becomes more a recording device than a teaching plan. I find that if I journal my observations and thoughts from each lesson, I am more able to reflect on what students have learned, to note all of their discoveries, and then apply and build on that learning in future activities. Keeping a journal is especially helpful if you are a specialist physical education teacher who sees many children and classes in a day.

I have found that students' ideas are more creative and innovative than mine would ever be. Even after coaching and teaching this sport for many years, I see different and unique ways of interpreting skills and completing tasks with each new group of students. In fact, I have found that the best learning occurs when students build off of their own ideas or the ideas of their classmates. One good idea leads to another good idea, which may inspire yet another extension of that movement concept. The learning curve never ends.

The Parts of a Lesson

Building a lesson should focus on three main parts: the introduction, the main body, and the closure. The introduction includes verbal instruction and physical activities that prepare the body *and* the mind for the forthcoming activities. Students need these mental and physical warm-up opportunities to ease into the transition from classroom to gymnasium.

Mental warm-up helps students understand where their focus will be and excites them for the class period ahead. For example, telling your students, "Today we will be exploring swings and circles with three different types

Safety	• Demonstrates the ability to move through general space safely
	• Demonstrates an understanding of personal space by respecting the personal space of others
	• Uses equipment properly
	• Works safely with equipment in personal space
	• Works effectively within general space
Group work	• Demonstrates a positive attitude toward peers
	• Works cooperatively with one other person
	• Works cooperatively with two or more people
	• Contributes ideas to group work
	• Communicates ideas
	• Demonstrates constructive and appropriate behavior for the setting and situation
	• Evaluates peers fairly and consistently
	• Is sensitive to student diversity and varied skill levels of others
Skill	• Is able to focus on a task and on development of specific skills.
	• Approaches learning challenges with different perspectives
	• Develops ideas and practices skills
	• Demonstrates mastery of basic skils
	• Can explain the fundamental elements for specific apparatuses
	• Is able to expand and elaborate on movement ideas
	• Is able to link skills into short sequences
	• Is able to link sequences together to make a routine
Attitude	• Demonstrates a positive attitude toward rhythmic gymnastics
	• Shows respect and cares for equipment
	• Is open to the ideas of others
	• Sets goals and works toward their attainment
	• Makes a connection across curricula when applicable
	• Builds self-challenge into routines
	• Shows initiative and creativity
Musicality	• Demonstrates an appreciation for a variety of musical styles
	• Is able to move and respond appropriately to selected music
	• Chooses suitable music for personal routines
	• Demonstrates understanding of beat, tempo, and rhythm
	• Demonstrates musical interpretation through movement
	• Derives pleasure and enjoyment from movement and music

Figure 5.1 Sample learning outcomes for rhythmic gymnastics.

of apparatus" will create anticipation. They will want to listen intently to what you have planned for them. It is also often helpful during the introduction to briefly review what was learned in the previous lesson: "You will remember that during the last class we used the ribbon for the first time and you saw the many different patterns it can make." This mental review will help students ready themselves for the physical activity ahead.

Physical warm-up prepares the body for activity. If students have just come from a sedentary class, they will need some time to adjust and attune their physical attentiveness. A good warm-up activity will raise internal body temperature and increase blood flow to all body parts and muscle groups. The best warm-up activities keep all students active and moving safely in their space. Thus, it is best not to use elimination games. Fast action games, with no-collision rules, can help to develop overall fitness and aerobic endurance as well as the ability to move safely amidst a group.

Warm-ups can also include exercises that focus on specific body parts. Flexibility exercises, for example, can be an important component of the warm-up in a rhythmic gymnastics program. Flexibility is simply the degree that you can move the body at a joint or the range of motion of a joint. In school-based rhythmic gymnastics, I focus primarily on hip and shoulder flexibility simply as a means of warming up joints to avoid injury and muscle strains. Anyone who has seen rhythmic gymnastics on television will appreciate that back and hip flexibility is important at the competitive level. In school-based rhythmic gymnastics, however, overexerting and overstretching the back are not recommended. Besides, schoolteachers have neither the time nor the expertise to properly train students in spinal flexibility. Instead, try to develop students' awareness and understanding of core stability. The muscles that support the spine should be equally strengthened so that they keep the spine aligned and maintain good posture.

The main body of the lesson can focus on everything from exploring or acquiring new skills to refining skills that have been previously learned. During this part of the lesson you may allow your students to explore what they can do with a new apparatus or challenge them with specific tasks and learning problems (see chapters 8 and 9). Students experienced in rhythmic gymnastics will likely work on developing their skill level and creating sequences or routines.

It is important to keep instructional time to a minimum during the main body of a lesson, both to ensure that students remain properly warmed up and to ensure that students get enough activity time. You will also want to allow time for students to practice their newly discovered movements. Ample exploration and practice time will help them master their newly acquired skills and will give them the time needed to understand the fundamental movement being covered. Practice will also give them time to gain the confidence they will need to demonstrate their sequences or skills in front of others.

Closure allows students the chance to prepare themselves for the transition from the gym back to the classroom. During this part of the lesson, quiet relaxation exercises work best. Relaxation helps students to calm down both physically and mentally. The closure period of a lesson is also a good opportunity to take a few moments to reflect on class performance and assess experiences. Finally, closure presents the perfect opportunity to let students know what to anticipate for the next class. Figure 5.2 provides a sample lesson plan outline. Use it to record your teaching plan and to keep track of the fundamental elements that have been covered for each apparatus.

Lesson Evaluation

As discussed earlier, lesson evaluation is an excellent way to prepare for future learning experiences. By asking some critical questions, teachers are able to evaluate the effectiveness of each lesson, as well as the overall program. At the end of each class time I take a few minutes to jot down some notes about what went well and what I would improve in future lessons. I ask myself, "Were the children truly engaged in their learning?" A few quick glances across the gym during class will usually have answered this question. If the children were active and involved, I consider the lesson a success.

Lesson # _____ General outcomes: ❐ Skills ❐ Safety ❐ Group work ❐ Routines

Date:		Class		Lesson focus	
Warm-up					
Space	❐ Personal ❐ General ❐ Direction ❐ Level ❐ Pathway ❐ Plane				
Body	❐ Jumps and leaps ❐ Locomotion ❐ Turns and pivots ❐ Balances				

		Rope	Hoop	Ball	Ribbon	Scarf	Other
Apparatuses	Fundamental elements	❐ Swing ❐ Jump and skip ❐ Rotate ❐ Wrap ❐ Throw and catch ❐ Release	❐ Swing ❐ Circle ❐ Roll – Floor ❐ Roll – body ❐ Spin ❐ Throw and catch ❐ Rotate ❐ Pass through or over	❐ Swing ❐ Circle ❐ Roll body ❐ Roll floor ❐ Bounce ❐ Figure 8 ❐ Throw and catch	❐ Swing ❐ Circle ❐ Spiral ❐ Figure 8 ❐ Snake	❐ Swing ❐ Circle ❐ Wave ❐ Figure 8 ❐ Throw and catch	❐ ❐ ❐ ❐

The Plan	❐ Direct teach ❐ Stations ❐ Circuit ❐ Partners ❐ Other _____
Closure	
Notes for next time	

Figure 5.2 Rhythmic gymnastics lesson plan form.

From *Teaching Rhythmic Gymnastics: A Developmentally Appropriate Approach* by Heather Palmer, 2003, Champaign, IL: Human Kinetics.

Another question to ask is whether each lesson builds on students' previous learning experiences. Are they expanding their knowledge base or are they learning random skills that lack connection and meaning? For example, swings and circles are fundamental elements for both the ribbon and the scarf. Thus, when I move from scarf to ribbon work, students have already had experience with scarf swings and circles. It's only a matter of applying these movement elements to a new apparatus, the ribbon.

Most importantly, I ask myself whether or not each student experienced some success. If children leave with a feeling of accomplishment, they will feel good about themselves and their confidence can only grow.

Incorporating Group Activities

The emphasis on group cooperation and learning is becoming a major focus in emerging physical education curricula. Through cooperative activities students are learning to work productively in group situations. Alberta [Canada] Learning considers student interaction so important that it is one of five general outcomes of the new year 2000 physical education curriculum. Students are encouraged through physical activity to communicate, demonstrate fair play, work well with others in various roles, and participate cooperatively in group activities.

Rhythmic gymnastics lends itself well to group activities. Students can work in pairs or small groups to add a new dimension to the rhythmic activities. Students can mirror each other as they create and perform routines. Having a partner to share in the fun makes the experience all the more enjoyable. I often give children the option of working alone or in a group and they will more often than not choose to work with other children. Children can still progress at their own speed but the collaboration and sharing that emerges during group work often helps a student go beyond what they would normally do if they were working alone. They gain confidence from the support they give to each other. Along with helping to build confidence, the interaction between students and

apparatus adds interest and variety to a rhythmic gymnastics sequence or routine. Students develop the ability to give and take as they agree on the skills that are to be included in the group routine. They also learn to compromise as they share the leadership role with other students.

For years we have understood the value of leadership qualities in students. We are now learning to appreciate that a good leader is also skilled in collaboration and cooperation. A good leader understands the importance of give-and-take and encourages the input of others' ideas. A good leader sometimes needs to step back and become a follower to allow the collaborative process to continue.

Summary

Before planning your rhythmic gymnastics lesson, it is important to identify what you want to accomplish with your group of students. Once you have established these learning outcomes, the lesson-planning process evolves naturally. By remaining flexible in the planning process, you will be better able to meet the diverse needs of your students and set a learning pace that is comfortable for everyone. Use an open-ended approach to allow for unexpected opportunities for enhanced learning.

The three-part lesson (including the introduction, the main body, and closure) is a tried-and-true method of organizing classroom instruction. Vital to this lesson plan in rhythmic gymnastics is limiting instructional time and maximizing activity time. Building in opportunities for exploration leads to creativity and freedom of expression. Including ample practice time helps students build confidence in their abilities and leads to skill mastery. When planning lessons, also try to include a balance of individual activities and opportunities for group interaction.

The best method for professional development is ongoing evaluation, including reflecting on students' learning. This evaluation need not be a long and involved process. In fact, it can be something as simple as asking, "Were the children involved in their learning?" and "Did the children experience success?" Share in your students' success and enjoy the learning along with them.

Chapter **6**

© Human Kinetics

Organizing for Teaching and Learning

There are many ways to organize an instructional setting to maximize learning opportunities. Whatever the method of class organization, the focus should be keeping students actively engaged by limiting instructional time and increasing activity time. There are many ways to organize a group for instruction of a rhythmic gymnastics unit. The way that you choose to organize your class will be highly dependent on what you hope to achieve within the class time and your own preferences as a teacher. This chapter also outlines some of the teaching methodologies or styles that are well suited to a rhythmic gymnastics program. The teaching style that you utilize will be influenced by how the class has been organized. For example, during whole-class instruction you may use a direct teaching style or present open-ended tasks and challenges. If students are rotating through stations for the first time, you would likely allow opportunities for free exploration. Whatever style you choose depends on your preference as a professional, your understanding of the learning needs of students, as well as your unique style.

Class Organization

There are several ways in which to organize a group of students for instruction or to facilitate their learning. How you organize your group will depend on what learning outcomes you hope they will achieve within a class time.

Whole-Class Instruction

Leading the class as a whole is a traditional method of teaching. In rhythmic gymnastics it can be used during warm-up or when directly teaching a new skill or concept. Whole-class instruction is useful when you are leading the entire group through learning challenges in chapters 8 and 9. Students can be placed in lines or rows, or they can place themselves in a random pattern. The teacher typically stands at the front of the group to deliver instruction or to present the learning challenge. Each person within the group is responding to the learning challenge you present in their own individual manner.

Half and Half

In the half-and-half organization of teaching, half of the class may be engaged in learning a task challenge or exploring a piece of equipment independently while the other half of the class is receiving direct instruction from the teacher. Partway through the class the groups switch. This teaching method enables teachers to instruct a smaller group of students while the second group is actively engaged in some activity. The drawback to this type of teaching is that teachers focus on the group being taught when their attention is needed to supervise the entire class. This method works well in a team-teaching situation when each teacher can be in charge of a group.

Stations

This type of class management is extremely practical when there are not enough apparatus for each student in class. With stations only a partial set of rhythmic gymnastics equipment is needed. Stations can be structured in a variety of ways. For example, each station can be stocked with a different type of equipment. Then students rotate through each station within a class period or other designated time frame. Another option is designating one station as the new skill station, where children are taught directly or guided by the teacher with tasks and challenges. The other stations can be designated for exploration or where students can work on routine building.

Circuits

In a circuit setup, the teacher organizes the equipment into a circular pattern around the gym. Students complete specific tasks at each station and quickly move on to the next to complete the circuit. For example, they may

jump in and out of hoops laid out flat on the floor,

bounce a ball five times,

jump over two outstretched ropes,

pick up a ribbon and create five circles,

toss a hoop onto a pylon,

skip five times,

do five different scarf swings and circles,

and so on around the stations until the time allowed is up.

Figure 6.1 illustrates a similar circuit. Circuits can also be set up for students to simply have fun doing a variety of activities. In this case, students would start at different points along the circuit to avoid delays or having to wait in line.

Individual Student Progress

This organizational structure works well for older students who are able to manage their own learning and initiate personal challenge. Using this method, students and teacher agree on a goal and students attempt to attain that goal. Some examples of goals may include:

- Complete a skills checklist. Students use individual checklists to record their progress, checking off those skills they have completed or demonstrated proficiently.
- Create a routine. Students work in groups to create a routine using new skills to be mastered. Each group works independently to achieve the goal of completing a routine.
- Teach a skill or sequence to the group: Students are assigned the task of creating a short sequence or developing a skill. Then they teach it to their peer group or to a group of younger students.

Partner and Group Work

Partner and group work develop positive social interaction between students. By collaborating to develop skills and build sequences or routines, students learn about social and group dynamics, including how to interact and cooperate with others. When using this type of class structure, encourage students to try different roles—for example, the idea person, the negotiator, the problem solver, the skill leader, and so on. By switching roles and responsibilities within a group, all students will have the opportunity to try out each leadership role.

This type of class management also optimizes children's strengths. For example, students can explore one-on-one relationships during

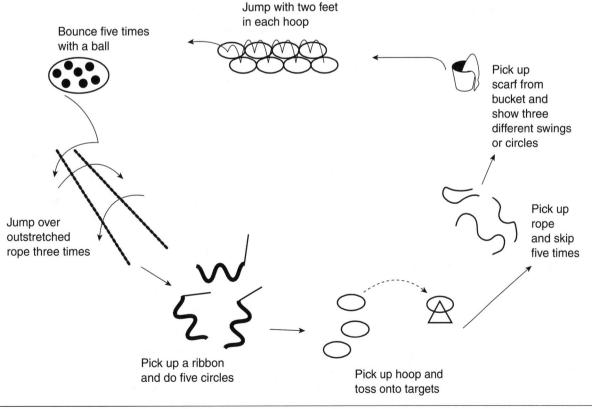

Figure 6.1 Apparatus set up in a circuit.

partnering. Children especially enjoy mirroring activities in which they face their partners and perform the movements as if they were looking into a mirror. In another technique, known as shadowing, students follow behind their partners and copy their movements. Such partner relationships become more complicated, and thus can be explored in even more depth, during group work.

Peer Teaching

You will discover that you have many students with unique talents that can be utilized to enhance the teaching and learning in a rhythmic gymnastics program. With this type of class management students are selected to demonstrate and explain newly discovered skills to classmates or to share their expertise (someone who is skilled at jump rope could share some of their tricks). This role should be shared among students over the course of the rhythmic gymnastics unit to allow as many students as possible the opportunity to become the "teacher." Or you can set up peer-teaching groups. Set up a group of three or four students and let children choose one skill that they would like to teach the other members of their group. This way each child has the opportunity to do some peer teaching in a relaxed and comfortable setting.

Teaching Methodology

Teaching methodology is the approach that you take to encourage learning in your students. It is your style of teaching. Several styles are presented here to help you enhance the learning of children and to vary your presentation style to maintain the interest of your students. The teaching methodology you choose will depend on the learning needs of your students as well as what you expect students to learn within each class. For example, if the goal of a particular lesson is to encourage a variety of creative responses, an open-ended task style will work well. If you are working with older students, want to introduce a specific skill, or want to introduce the specifics of a skill, direct teaching may be best.

You will find that the open-ended task approach brings about more creativity and innovation in movement. The most important benefit of an educational movement approach is that you do not need technical expertise about the sport of rhythmic gymnastics; rather you can simply facilitate dynamic and motivating learning experiences.

Free Exploration and Discovery

Children of all ages need the opportunity to explore using their bodies and apparatus. With free exploration and discovery, students are free to explore using their apparatus within a few parameters, such as selection of available equipment. No other limits are put on them, with the exception of safety guidelines (e.g., "Use the ribbons in your own space and hide the end of the stick in the palm of your hand to prevent poking others or yourself."). Rather, creativity and open discovery are the goals. Ample time for exploration is especially important when children are introduced to a new activity or apparatus for the first time. Through the process of free exploration and discovery children will gain confidence in their abilities as they develop their skills at their own pace. These feelings of success will enable them to challenge themselves in future activities in rhythmic gymnastics.

Offer free exploration and discovery opportunities frequently, even for older students. These learning opportunities capitalize on students' natural desire to move and create. Even in adult workshops I provide adult learners with ample opportunity to discover and explore. This method of self-discovery is an important aspect of learning and allows individuals to explore their creative potential.

Guided Exploration and Discovery

With this teaching method the teacher has a predetermined idea of the learning outcomes of each lesson. As with free exploration and discovery, certain parameters are set, such as equipment selection. But in guided exploration and discovery, the teacher guides students toward desired learning outcomes using some key words to help them with their exploration. Key phrases and prompts will help students to expand their own movement potential. For example: "Listen to the music and try to make your ribbon follow the music." "Keep your ribbon light and full of air." This style is similar to open-ended, task-based learning but allows far more time for exploration and discovery.

Direct Teaching

Direct teaching is a teacher-centered approach and entails teaching specific skills in a direct manner. Students are taught a skill using the correct progressions and are then allowed to practice the skill. Basic skills are mastered before more complex skills are introduced. In this way students experience greater success at skill mastery.

The teacher provides specific instruction. For example, the instructor might say, "Last week we worked on different types of circles with the ribbon. This week we are going to learn a sagittal figure 8, which is a circle at each side of the body." This style of teaching limits creativity, but it can be useful when teaching a more complex skill with several progressions leading up to it or when trying to refine skills and movements.

Open-Ended Tasks and Problem Solving

With this method the teacher presents a potential learning situation as a problem that needs to be solved. That is, a variety of tasks and challenges are presented to lead students through the problem-solving process. For example: "How many different ways can you bounce the ball?" "Can you bounce the ball in a different position other than standing?"

When presenting tasks and challenges to children, I choose my words carefully to ensure that they come up with their own solutions and movement ideas. I avoid using phrases such as "show me" or "I would like to see" because this type of instruction will make students want to please me rather than explore their own movement potential. Encouraging

individual work and problem solving, on the other hand, will guide students toward discovering that there are no correct solutions to these movement problems and, thus, that their own ideas are valuable and worth considering. And, students will begin doing the movements for themselves instead of trying to please the teacher.

The following prompts will help you present problems in an open-ended manner and will encourage students to work together and show one another what they can do.

- "Discover different ways to . . ."
- "Can you . . . ?"
- "Explore how many different ways you can . . ."
- "Try to make the [apparatus] . . ."
- "See how many times you can . . ."
- "Try to move like a . . ."
- "Can you move yourself and your [apparatus] to the sound of . . . ?"
- "Show that you can use both your left and right sides to . . ."
- "Try to put . . . [two or more] skills together into a sequence."
- "Find another way to show the same movement at a different level."
- "See if you can do the same movement with . . . [a different apparatus]."
- "Continue the same movement and then try to add . . ."
- "Can you create a pattern using . . . ?"
- "Do the same skill, but this time use a different pathway."
- "Try the same movement at a different speed."

I also like to promote cooperation by phrasing tasks in a way that encourages students to share movement ideas with one another. For example, I might ask students to show their classmates all the different ways they can perform a certain skill (e.g., roll a hoop). I will often have half the group share their movement ideas while the other half watches, and then switch. This gives everyone the opportunity to enjoy the experience of having an audience.

Summary

How you organize students for instruction will be a personal choice. Choose what suits your personal teaching style and your educational setting. Some skills will require that you organize the class into whole-class instruction for direct teaching. When first introducing students to an apparatus, using stations works very well. The teaching methodology that most often suits the nature of rhythmic gymnastics is an open-ended approach in which students find their own solution to problem-solving challenges. This approach promotes a variety of responses and helps to elicit creativity in students. Whatever organizational style or teaching methodology you choose, let your instincts be your guide and let your own personal style shine through.

Choosing Music

Music plays a vital role in the overall rhythmic gymnastics experience. Music will stimulate ideas for movement and inspire creativity within students. The right music selection will set the mood for the learning environment and connote the feeling and theme of the lesson. In an introductory lesson on skipping skills, for example, peppy, energetic music would work well. If introducing the scarf and swinging motions, you would likely select music with a smooth, flowing, even tempo.

Selecting music can be a difficult and expensive process, but I have found some ways to make it easier. For example, I often visit the public library to listen to different types of music. To make my music selection right on the spot, I take my own portable system into the library. Once I find some interesting songs, I try to locate the CDs at a music store and buy them. If your library doesn't have a wide selection of different types of music, many of the larger music stores have listening stations where you can hear an entire CD, or portions of it, before you purchase it. Music stores also make it easy to find specific types of music by grouping CDs into certain categories. Instrumental sound tracks and music designed specifically for educational movement activities are often the most useful. Another option is to have students bring in their favorite music from home; however, be sure to screen it for appropriateness (e.g., language, positive and respectful gender portrayal) before using it in class.

In my years of teaching I have compiled various music selections on audiotape, and have recently copied them onto a CD. (CDs are much more convenient for class instruction because you can quickly move from one track to the next, as opposed to having to wait for a tape to rewind or fast forward.) I keep several of my favorite CDs in a case that stays right in the gym, ready for any class, be it rhythmic gymnastics, movement, games, or dance. I am also generous with my music, sharing it with my colleagues whenever they ask. And they, in turn, share their favorite music compilations with me! I get exposed to a wider selection of music choices and my collection of good movement music grows.

This chapter discusses the consideration involved when selecting music for a rhythmic gymnastics unit such as age of participants and including variety in your choice of music selection and the importance of exposing children to a variety of musical genres. Suggestions are given on how to select music that is appropriate for the various apparatus and how to relate the chosen movements to the music. Uses of percussion instruments such as tambourines are included as good accompaniment to movement and rhythmic gymnastics skills. The final section of this chapter discusses basic music terminology.

Age of Participants

When selecting music, consider the age of your students. A song with a varied tempo and rhythm will be more difficult for younger children to follow. Instead, choose music with a steady tempo and beat. Younger children will enjoy familiar tunes from television shows and movies, while older students may want something modern—for example, songs they hear on the radio and on music video channels.

Music sets the stage for rhythmic gymnastics movement, which should be joyful and fun. For younger children choose uplifting music with melodies that are not too melancholy or monotonous. Because their response time is still developing, younger children may also need music with a slower beat. For example, young students will need more time because they will be bouncing and catching the ball using two hands. Older students, on the other hand, will be completing a series of one-handed rhythmic bounces to music.

The sophistication of the music will also be a factor. For younger children the more obvious the beat, the easier it will be to communicate that beat through movement. An orchestral piece may seem too large and grandiose for a group of first-graders, but older students performing larger movements would do this type of music justice. The music must not overpower the movements; nor should a strong performance overpower the music.

Variety

No matter what the age and musical tastes of my students, I take the opportunity to expose them to a variety of music genres and musical artists, including pop, rock, jazz, blues, country, seasonal, "techno," classical, and cultural music. I especially enjoy playing a familiar classical piece (e.g., "Beethoven's Fifth") and having students tell me, "Hey, I know that song." It is wonderful that so many familiar classical pieces are used on movie, television, and commercial soundtracks. They are becoming part of present-day culture.

Variety can also mean choosing pieces that highlight various instruments. Classical music, for example, does not always have to be played by an orchestra. Exposing children to instrumental pieces such as classical guitar, piano, violin, and other single instruments can initiate a new idea for rhythmic movement. By exposing children to a variety of pieces, you will maintain their interest while at the same time fostering their understanding and appreciation of music.

Apparatus

Music selection specific to each apparatus is a matter of personal choice. Music with a good melody will likely be appropriate for all apparatus. But there are some general guidelines that will help you select music for each specific piece of equipment.

- For the ball, and bouncing activities in particular, choose music with a fairly fast tempo and a definite beat.
- For the ribbon, music should be melodic and communicate flow, grace, and gentle movement. To promote and encourage a continuous, cohesive ribbon pattern, the music should have a weak beat. Music selections used for the ribbon will also suit scarves, large or small.
- For the scarf, select music with soft and airy melodies.
- Music for the rope should have energetic, staccato rhythms for jumping activities as well as smooth, flowing melodies for swings and other soft movements.

- For the hoop, music selection is often the easiest. The hoop works well with many types of music with a moderate tempo.

It's helpful to keep brief notes about each song on a CD or tape—for example, "slow, moderate tempo," "fast," and so on. You might also note specific lesson themes, such as "good for ball bouncing," "good for flowing movements," and so on. These notes will provide a quick reference of suitable songs for each teaching situation. When choosing music keep in mind that high notes are often interpreted through light movements at a high level, and low notes tend to connote heavy movements performed low to the ground.

When listening to a piece of music in preparation for use in rhythmic gymnastics instruction, ask yourself the following questions. You might also want to try the music in class to see how students respond.

- Does the music convey a specific movement (e.g., swing, circle, or roll)?
- What type of movements can you visualize the students performing to this type of music? Will they be soft and flowing or energetic and upbeat?
- Does the music build and add excitement?
- Does it motivate you to move?
- Does it have a discernable rhythm that is predictable and easy to follow?
- Do any themes emerge from this music (e.g., a flowing river, a space creature, sounds of a rainforest)?
- Is the sound recording of good enough quality to project across a gym?
- Do you like the music? Do you think your students will like the music?

Percussion Alternatives

Tambourines and other percussion instruments such as the drum can be used instead of recorded music to communicate movement ideas. The tambourine can create two distinct sounds. When shaken the tambourine conveys a sustained movement. Striking the tambourine makes a great staccato sound that conveys a stop in movement or truncated, jerky movements. The tambourine can also be used to signal group changes, such as starting, stopping, and switching direction. Gradually increasing the speed of drumbeats and other percussive sounds can guide students' movements from slow to fast. Varying drumbeat intensity can convey heavy and light movements.

Students can also create their own percussion instruments and use them as hand apparatus during their routines to create their own music. Rhythm sticks, tambourines, shakers, and drums can be made easily from paper plates, plastic containers, tubes, and other common materials. Creating a rhythmic routine using percussion instruments as alternative apparatus is optimizing the students' involvement as they are involved in the creation of the apparatus, through to the use of the apparatus as part of a sequence or routine.

Basic Musical Terms

Rhythmic gymnastics, as its name implies, integrates musical rhythms with physical movement. The innate connection between body rhythms and musical rhythms naturally emerges when students interpret music through movement. To guide students in discovering this marriage between music and movement, a basic understanding of music terminology is needed.

The following terms and definitions are presented for those who wish to learn about or review music terminology. By understanding these terms, you will be better able to assist your students in expanding their knowledge of and appreciation for music.

• Rhythm is the controlled movement of music through time, just as rhythmic gymnastics is the controlled movement of the body through time. Rhythm can be described as organized groupings of sounds and pauses, which create patterns. Marching music, for example is usually four counts grouped together with the emphasis on the first count. Waltz music is three counts with the emphasis placed on the first beat. Students can demonstrate their understanding of rhythm by performing an element to match the rhythm of the music. If the accent or emphasis in a piece of music is on the first count out of four counts, the student might demonstrate this by bouncing, followed by three walking steps.

• Beat is the rhythmic pulse heard and felt in a musical composition. If you find yourself tapping your foot to the music, you will likely be tapping out the beat. The pulsation of beat can be easily interpreted into movement. Percussion instruments, the drum in particular, often mark the beat heard behind, or in the background of, the melody. In rhythmic gymnastics, students can demonstrate their understanding of beat by bouncing the ball, swinging the ribbon rhythmically, clapping, or performing repetitious skips of the rope.

• A tone or beat that is emphasized over another is an accent. An accented beat is louder or longer than other beats. To help students hear the accented beat, listen to a piece of music and then clap on the strongest beat. For example, in a four-beat rhythm with the first beat accented, students would clap the following pattern: clap, 2, 3, 4, clap, 2, 3, 4, and so on. They will soon discover that there will be an equal number of beats between each accent and that the pattern can be interpreted with different body or apparatus elements. In rhythmic gymnastics, students might interpret accent by putting more emphasis on that movement. For example, a student might bounce a ball forcefully on the accent and lightly on the unaccented beats.

• Beats are grouped together in a single measure. In a three-beat rhythm a measure comprises three beats; in a four-beat rhythm, four beats constitute a single measure. In the four-beat rhythm described in the previous paragraph, the accent is on the first beat of each measure. On sheet music vertical lines separate each measure.

• A phrase is a short musical sequence, or passage, complete in itself. This sequence comprises a single thought or idea in music, similar to a sentence in writing. In vocal music a phrase will likely be a single verse. A short rhythmic sequence can include two or three phrases of a song. Students can interpret a phrase in rhythmic gymnastics by keeping the movements similar within the phrase and then changing the movement during the next phrase. For example a student may perform swinging motions with the apparatus for the entire phrase. When a new phrase begins, their movements can change to a different element such as circling, to reflect the change in the music.

• Tempo is simply the pace, or rate of speed, of music. It can be described as fast, slow, or moderate. Students can easily interpret tempo through their movement by matching what they do with the apparatus to the speed of the music. For example, when skipping with the rope, the students listen for the beat, which will dictate the tempo, and jump over the rope for every beat that they hear.

Summary

Music is the key component of a high-quality rhythmic gymnastics program. It can create a mood, inspire an idea, and stimulate creative movement themes. Music is very much a part of society and is enjoyed by all. Thus, by including music in your rhythmic gymnastics instruction, you will be not only adding to your students' enjoyment of the sport but also enhancing their total learning experience.

The right music selection will stimulate students' movement responses. Begin building your music collection over time until you have a repertoire of music, from a variety of genres, appropriate for rhythmic gymnastics. The challenge will be choosing the best piece of music for each apparatus; however, if you choose music with a good melody and a predictable tempo, it will likely work well with any apparatus. When possible, include opportunities to work with percussion instruments, especially when exploring rope skills (e.g., skipping) and ball skills (e.g., bouncing). The best way to learn about these music concepts is through physical movement and apparatus manipulation, or essentially, moving to the music.

Part Two

Incorporating Learning Experiences Into the Rhythmic Gymnastics Unit

Chapter **8**

© Helen Scott Studios

Spatial Awareness and Movement

The ability of students to move and control their bodies safely is a starting point for rhythmic gymnastics and many of the related skills. When students are able to control their body movements they can expand their skills and, thus, experience greater mastery when hand apparatus are added. The use of proper progressions, such as first trying a skill without the apparatus and then adding the apparatus, will help to ensure that students receive the proper foundation for future learning.

Spatial awareness activities are not only important for young students. Older students, whose bones and muscles are also still growing, will continue to need ongoing spatial awareness and movement activities as they adjust to their developing muscles and lengthening limbs. Spatial awareness includes personal and general space as well as the different directions the body travels and the various pathways, planes, and levels through which the body and apparatus move.

There are fundamental body elements specific to rhythmic gymnastics that can be incorporated into a school program. These include balances (i.e., static positions), locomotion (e.g., running, skipping, hopping), turns and pivots, and jumps and leaps. These body elements are fundamental to overall student growth and development, and are an integral component of a rhythmic gymnastics program.

This chapter explains each of these movement concepts in basic terms and suggests teaching tips and learning challenges to assist students in developing spatial awareness and learning the fundamental body elements in rhythmic gymnastics. The next chapter expands on these concepts with the addition of hand apparatus.

Spatial Awareness

Some teachers introduce spatial awareness activities only at the beginning of the year, but body awareness should be part of any lesson, be it rhythmic gymnastics or sport-related games and activities. The ability to control their body movements and move safely within personal and general space will help students in whatever physical activity they pursue in life.

▶ Personal and General Space

Spatial awareness can be classified into two groups: personal space and general or common space. Personal space is the area immediately around the student, whereas general space is the larger common space used by a group of students (e.g., open field, gym, dance studio).

Teaching Tips

- Encourage students to keep their eyes open and their heads up when moving through common space.
- The goals of personal and general space activities are for students to learn how to share space with other students and to move safely through a space without hurting others or themselves.

Learning Challenges

- Students find a space in the gym where they are not touching anyone or anything. Once they have found a position, students should look around to familiarize themselves with their "home space." On your command, students run toward any wall, touch it, and return to their home space. Try the same activity again, but instead of touching a wall, students should move anywhere in the open space in a prescribed way (e.g., walk, hop, or run in place) and then return to their home space at the signal.

- Students explore moving around the common space using different body parts. Have them travel using one foot, both feet, one hand and one foot, and so on. At the signal, students freeze, holding their position. At the next signal, they start moving again, this time using a different body part.

- In groups of four, students establish a group home space. At the signal, each student runs toward a different corner of the common space. They touch their corners and then return to their group home space. You can also have student groups travel together, holding hands, and touch each wall without bumping into other groups.

- Students quickly learn how to group themselves into set squads in this activity. At your command (e.g., "Groups of two!"), students find partners and sit in an empty space. At your next command (e.g., "Groups of four!"), partners link up with another pair and find an empty space to sit. A command such as "On your own!" will mean students have to break out of their groups and find their own personal space. This is a great activity for developing students' listening skills.

▶ Directions

Directions are the routes students take while moving through personal or common space. Directions include forward, backward, sideways, and diagonal.

Teaching Tips

- Body position determines direction.
- Help students understand direction in terms of their body position within a space (e.g., your nose leads you forward, your back leads you backward, upward is toward the sky, downward is toward the ground).
- Help students understand geographical direction by using the commands north, south, east, and west.

Learning Challenges

- Have students explore directions by traveling in different ways and on different body parts in each of the directions. For example, show how to travel forward or backward with three body parts touching the ground (e.g., both hands and one foot).

- Label each wall of the gym with the appropriate geographical direction: north, south, east, and west. For older students, include northwest, southwest, northeast, and southeast directions. At your signal, students must travel to the correct wall or corner safely without touching anyone else. The object of this activity is not to get there the quickest but to get to the correct location without touching anyone or being touched.

- Students will become proficient at changing direction quickly and accurately with this activity. Use a tambourine or drum instead of a voice command. At the signal, students move in a specified way. At the next signal, students change direction and their method of travel. For example, they may change from skipping forward to hopping sideways.

- In this activity students create a traveling sequence using three different movements in three different directions. They begin in a static (balance) position. At the signal, they move in one direction using a specific movement. At the next signal, they move in another direction using a different movement. At the next signal, they move in yet another direction using yet another movement. They finish the sequence with a static balance.

- In pairs, students imagine that they are repelling magnets. There is an invisible force that keeps them face to face within an arm's length of each other. One partner is designated the leader. At your signal, leaders slowly move in one direction and their partners follow them to maintain the face-to-face position. Followers must try to anticipate the leaders' movements to maintain the correct distance. This is a cooperative activity. Leaders are not trying to get away from their partners; rather, they are trying to lead them through the general space using different directions. Try the same activity exploring different pathways, and have students change roles so that everyone gets the opportunity to be the leader.

▶ Pathways

Pathways are movements and travel routes through general space. Pathways may be curved, figure 8s, straight, zigzag, or angular. Pathways can also be shapes, such as triangles, squares, and circles. Figure 8.1 illustrates examples of pathways. Pathways can be combined together to make pathway patterns (e.g., travel in figure 8 pattern followed by a straight path and finishing with a zigzag pattern). In rhythmic gymnastics, students can use pathways to make their sequences and movements more interesting. Spiraling a ribbon while standing in one spot on the floor may be an appropriate skill for a younger student, but an older student can add to this skill by performing ribbon spirals while skipping in a spiral pathway to create an interesting and dynamic visual picture.

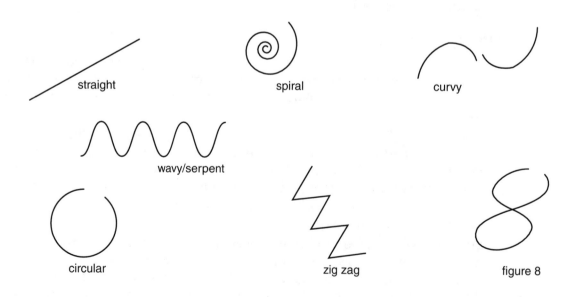

Figure 8.1   Pathways for movement of the body or the apparatus.

Teaching Tips

- Use imagery to help students understand the concept of pathways.
- Use contrasting terms to emphasize the different movement pathways such as zigzag and straight.
- Use obstacles, such as beanbags and pylons, and have students move around the obstacles to demonstrate various pathways.

Learning Challenges

- Either during class time or gym time map out some different pathways using a pencil and paper. Combine this activity with an art lesson about the different kinds of lines used to create images.

- Have students create their own pathway maps. Ask them to combine three pathways into a sequence, then map their pathways on paper. Figure 8.2 shows an example of a three-pathway map. Then students can exchange pathway maps with one another and try moving according to their new pathway map.

Figure 8.2 Example of a three-pathway map.

▶ Levels

A level defines the relationship of the body to the floor. Squatting, sitting, and lying are considered low levels. Standing and crouching are considered medium levels, and rising, jumping, and stretching upward are considered high levels.

Teaching Tips

- Encourage students to explore levels beyond the basics. Rather than walk tall at a high level, for example, students jump into the air to reach a higher level.
- Levels can also be communicated with sound. A high sound designates a high-level movement and a low sound communicates a low-level movement.

Learning Challenges

- Help young students discover levels by using imagery. Ask them to show the movements of low-lying animals such as snakes, alligators, turtles, and lizards. Then have them mimic the movements of a dog, bear, or wolf to demonstrate a medium level. A soaring hawk or a jumping kangaroo could be used to show a high-level movement.
- Begin with children lying flat on the floor. At a slow count to 10, students rise to the standing position. (They should not reach the standing position before they reach 10.) Then have them count backward while returning to a low position on the floor.
- In this mirroring activity the lead students move to different levels while their partners try to follow. Again the focus is on cooperation. The follower is trying to match their movements to the leader as they move their bodies to different levels.

- Play a game of musical hoops using static balances at different levels. Arrange enough hoops on the floor for the number of students in class. When the music starts students travel around the hoops using a specific movement (e.g., skipping, tiptoeing, walking). When the music stops students find any hoop and maintain a static position (balance) at a certain level (e.g., high, medium). When the music starts again, students continue traveling around the hoops in another direction and using a different movement, followed by a static balance, and so on.

▶ Planes

Planes are the spaces in which an apparatus or the body can travel (figure 8.3). When skills are performed in the proper plane they appear logical and are visually aesthetic. Skills performed in an improper plane, known as out of plane, appear random and messy. The frontal plane is vertical. It is the space immediately in front or behind the body. For example, passing through a door would be passing through the vertical plane. The sagittal plane is on either side of the body, often called the "wheel." The horizontal plane is parallel to the horizon.

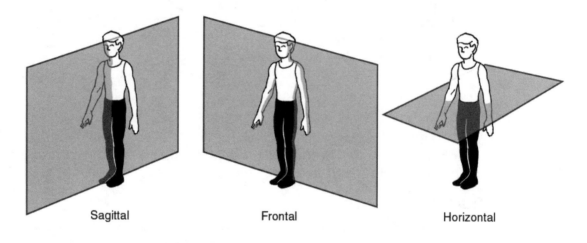

Sagittal   Frontal   Horizontal

Figure 8.3   Frontal, horizontal, and sagittal planes.

Planes are a rather abstract concept and may be difficult for young students to understand. When they experience planes kinesthetically, however, they soon grow to understand the concept. I frequently use familiar words to describe planes to young children, making reference to the side of the body I want them to use. For example, I might request that they try moving the apparatus overhead or around the body (horizontal plane), at the side of the body (sagittal plane), or in front of the body (frontal plane). For older students the challenge will be making smooth transitions from one plane to the next when creating a sequence or routine. Figure 8.4 provides suggestions on how the different planes can be demonstrated using rhythmic gymnastics apparatus.

Plane	Word prompts	How to demonstrate
Frontal	"door"	Large circle with ribbon in front of body.
		Rotate half-fold rope in front of body.
		Rotate a hoop on hand held in front of body.
Sagittal	"wheel"	Large circle with ribbon at either side of body.
		Rotate half-fold rope at either side of body.
		Rotate a hoop on hand at either side of body.
Horizontal	"table"	Large circle with ribbon overhead.
		Rotate half-folded rope overhead.
		Rotate hoop around body (hula).

Figure 8.4 Demonstrating planes with different apparatus.

Teaching Tips

- Planes are best demonstrated or explained using hand apparatus.
- Planes are an advanced rhythmic gymnastics concept. Younger students simply need to know that apparatus can be moved at their sides, in front of them, and around them.

Learning Challenges

- Fold a rope in half. Rotate the rope in front of the body a waist height to show the frontal plane. Rotate the rope overhead to show the horizontal plane. Rotate the rope at the side of the body to show the sagittal (side) plane.
- Lay hoops on the floor in a random pattern. At your command, students pass through the hoops in the prescribed plane. At the "frontal plane" command, they pass forward through the hoop. The "horizontal plane" command means they step into the hoop and lift it overhead, keeping it horizontal to the floor. At the "sagittal [or side] plane" command, students step sideways through the hoop.

Movement Cards

To reinforce the concepts of direction, pathway, and level, create a set of movement cards that show students the level, direction, and pathway they must travel with their bodies. Allow a student to select a card and read the commands that are depicted on the card to the group. Figure 8.5 shows you examples of movement cards. More cards can be created using different combinations of level, pathway, and direction.

High	Forward, straight ———————
Medium	
Low	

High	
Medium	Backward, zigzag ∧∧∧
Low	

High	
Medium	
Low	Sideways, curvy ⌒

Figure 8.5 Examples of movement cards.

Fundamental Body Elements

Fundamental body elements, including locomotion, jumps and leaps, pivots and turns, and static balances, should first be explored without apparatus. Later, when body mastery has been achieved, the addition of apparatus heightens the challenge as students learn to move their bodies at the same time they are manipulating an apparatus.

▶ Locomotion

Locomotion is moving the body from one space to another. Locomotion includes walking, running, galloping, skipping, hopping, and any other movement that moves the body from one place to another. In rhythmic gymnastics, locomotion is combined with apparatus skills to add challenge and interest to tasks, and to make sequences and routines more challenging and interesting. Combining two skills, such as bouncing a ball and galloping, extends the learning and heightens the level of difficulty. Thus, it is best to follow a logical progression, ensuring that each locomotion skill is learned independently before adding an apparatus. Always ensure that students wear proper footwear for any locomotion activities. Locomotion skills are important in the development of children's large muscle capabilities. Developing locomotion skills not only benefits a child's overall development but will also boost future performance in physical activities and sports.

Walking

Walking is the simple task of placing one foot in front of the other and shifting weight. In rhythmic gymnastics a walk is executed with the head held upright, the back kept tall and aligned, and the arms swung in natural, alternating movements. The foot and toe are fully extended (pointed), flexed, or in a relaxed natural state. The foot can come in contact with the floor in a heel-toe or toe-heel pattern. Walking is a flowing and natural rhythmic movement.

Teaching Tips

- Encourage students to hold their bodies straight and tall when walking to help them develop a sense of core stability.
- Slowly add other locomotion skills to increase fitness. For example, gradually build up from walking to running.
- Students must learn to listen to their bodies. If they become tired, they should slow down their movement rather than stopping abruptly.

Learning Challenges

- Students practice walking on tiptoe, alternating between one heel and one toe, and walking on two heels. Combine these walking methods to create a walking pattern (e.g., four steps on toes, four steps on heels, four steps on toes, and so on).
- Students walk to a rhythmic beat, set by a percussion instrument or music with a strongly emphasized beat.
- Students practice walking at different levels. For example, have them walk low to the ground, their hands nearly dragging on the floor. Then have them walk high and tall with their arms stretching upward.

- Have students walk as they would if trying to move through sticky syrup, hot sand, sticky mud, and deep snow.
- Students take giant steps and then small steps. When taking giant steps, students should become as large as they can be. Likewise, students should crouch down to become as small as possible when taking small steps.
- Students show different emotions through walking. For example, how would they walk if they were sad? Happy? Tired? Energetic?
- Students create a movement pattern with their arms while walking. For example, they straighten their arms, then bend them, then cross them, then straighten them, then bend them, and so on.
- Students walk around the gym. At your signal, they change direction and walk using a different pathway. Use a percussion instrument (e.g., tap on a drum) to indicate each direction change.

Running

Running, like walking, is the transfer of weight from one foot to the other, but running entails a greater stride and height. Running activities are important for fitness development and can be integrated into warm-up activities. In rhythmic gymnastics a rhythmic run is a light energetic stride usually performed to music. The feet contact the floor on the beat of the music. Often the legs and toes kick upward and backward, with the toes pointed. The arms swing naturally at the side of the body.

Teaching Tips

- Students should run on the balls of their feet with the heel touching the floor only momentarily.
- Tell students to keep their heads up and looking forward.
- The arms and upper body should be relaxed while running, and the arms should swing naturally forward and backward.
- Always ensure that students wear proper footwear for any locomotion activities.

Learning Challenges

- Students run around the perimeter of the gym and then change direction at the signal.
- Students alternate between a run and a walk. They can run for 10 counts and then walk for 5. Or they can create their own running/walking pattern that suits their personal fitness level.
- Students run forward, sideways, or backward (remind students to check behind them).
- Students run with a partner by linking arms, holding hands, or running side by side in unison.
- Students run to a rhythmic beat. Start by running for three counts and on the fourth count jump with both feet together. Continue the pattern: Run, 2, 3, jump, run, 2, 3, jump, and so on. Then have students create new run-jump patterns.
- Students run with their knees high in the air and tap their knees with their hands.
- Alternate four running strides with four walking steps.
- Students run on the spot and, on signal, walk to a new spot and begin running in place until the next signal.
- Place pylons or obstacles on the floor and have students run around them.

Skipping and Galloping

Galloping comes quite naturally to children. Galloping is a step-together, step-together motion performed in rapid succession. The same leg leads with each gallop. Gallops can be performed forward or sideways. In rhythmic gymnastics a gallop is performed with energy and elevation. The legs push off the ground and come together in the air. Skipping is similar to galloping, except it is a step-hop motion performed with alternating legs. The right legs steps forward, the left knee lift while the right foot hops. Then the left leg steps forward and the right knee lifts and the left foot hops. Some children will skip naturally while other need to have this skill broken down and then practiced at a slow speed. The rhythmic gymnastics skip is light, energetic, and airy. The arms swing naturally in opposition at the sides of the body.

Teaching Tips

- Be sure the same foot stays forward when galloping.
- Younger students will likely find it easier to gallop than to skip.
- Students can skip backward or in a turning pattern.

Learning Challenges

- Students try to gallop like a horse.
- Have students gallop/skip following different pathways.
- Students gallop/skip with a light, airy feeling, then with a heavy, thick feeling.
- In pairs, students gallop/skip forward toward their partners and then backward away from their partner.
- Students gradually increase and then decrease their speed as they skip or gallop.
- In small groups, have students gallop sideways in a circle.
- Have students try galloping leading with both their right and left legs.

► Leaping and Jumping

Jumps and leaps are considered fundamental elements in rhythmic gymnastics. For a school-based program, activities involving jumping and leaping will develop students' strength and cardiovascular fitness. A jump is performed with a two-foot take-off and a two-foot landing. A leap is performed by taking off with one foot and landing on the other. The knees and ankles help to absorb a jump by bending. Jumping and leaping are particularly fun for students when there are challenges and obstacles to overcome.

Teaching Tips

- Students should increase the height of their jump/leap by using their arms, swinging them forward and upward.
- Encourage students to land with control. Landings should always be absorbed by the feet, ankles, and knees.

Learning Challenges

- Students practice jumping and turning in the air, using their arms to gain height and to rotate their bodies. Begin with a quarter turn, then a half turn, then a three-quarters turn, and then a full turn. Call out directions such as front, back, left, and right.

- Scatter beanbags around the floor. Have students jump over the beanbags as they are traveling with two-foot jumps.
- Have students try a tuck jump, tapping their knees in the air. Then challenge them to complete a series of tuck jumps.
- Jump from a high level and finish at a low level. Jump from a low level and finish at a high level. For example, student might begin at a low level in a squat and jump and land at a tall level like standing.
- Play music and have students jump to the beat. Create a jumping pattern that resembles hopscotch (i.e., one foot, one foot, two feet, one foot).
- Have students count how many jumps it takes to travel from one side of the gym to the other.
- Scatter hoops in a random formation on the floor. Students travel around the gym using a specified movement. When they come to a hoop, they jump in and out with two feet and continue on their way. Students can count how many hoops they jump into within the time permitted.
- Stretch ropes straight out on the floor and have students travel in prescribed ways (e.g., hop, jump, leap, skip, etc.) around the gym. When students come to a rope they must leap over the rope from one foot to the next (figure 8.6). A variation of this activity is to create a "creek" using two ropes stretched out side by side on the floor. At one end the creek is narrow (i.e., the ropes are close together), and at the other end the creek is wider (i.e., the ropes are farther apart). Students count how many times they can jump or leap across the "creek" within the time permitted.

Figure 8.6 Leaping the "creek."

▶ Static Positions (Balances)

A static position, or balance, is a pose that is held long enough to show a defined shape in space. Students can create a balance on various body parts that serve as a base. There are many balances in rhythmic gymnastics; figure 8.7 shows some examples of static positions, both individual and with partners. Students will freely discover these static positions on their own.

Individual   With partners

a   b

Figure 8.7   Static positions *(a)* for individuals and *(b)* for partners.

Teaching Tips

- To add variety, have students create static balances with a partner.
- Encourage students to hold a static balance for three seconds.

Learning Challenges

- Students use a prescribed movement to travel around the gym to music. When the music stops they must show a static position. Positions may include three body parts touching the ground; a low, medium, or high balance; a balance with two students working together, and so on.
- Encourage students to explore balances other than those done on the feet.
- Students hold a static position on one leg and change the position of the free leg to various positions (e.g., bent in front, straight out in front, behind the back with a bent knee, straight back) without losing their balance.
- Focusing on one spot can help students maintain good balance. Try this activity. Have students create a balance. While they hold it ask students to look around the gym. Try the same balance again but this time have students focus on a certain spot on the wall. Maintaining focus on one spot will help them maintain their balance.

▶ Pivoting and Turning

Turns and pivots simply involve rotating the body to a different orientation. That is, the entire body rotates during pivots and turns. In a pivot one foot stays firmly planted on the ground while the other foot moves freely in a clockwise or counterclockwise direction around the pivot point (the planted foot). In a turn both feet move freely. Turns can also be done with different body parts—for example, rotating on the buttocks or turning the torso from front to back while lying on the floor.

Teaching Tips

- Remind students to rotate in both directions.
- Encourage students to keep their balance, and avoid getting too dizzy, by turning only once before turning in the other direction.
- Introduce the full turn, three-quarter turn, half turn, and quarter turn early on.

Learning Challenges

- Students find a spot on the floor and plant one foot. The other foot is free to travel clockwise or counterclockwise.
- Introduce to children directional turns such as full turn, three-quarter turn, half turn, and quarter turn. Have children scattered in a random pattern on the floor but all facing one direction. On command have student respond to your instructions such as one-quarter turn to the right. One-half turn to the right. This is a good activity for practicing listening and following instructions.
- In pairs, students stand facing their partners and holding hands. They swing their arms to one side and overhead, turning their bodies under their hands until they are back to back. Then repeat this same movement so that student partners are facing each other once again (figure 8.8). Some may know this movement as "wash the dishes," "dry the dishes," or "turn the dishes over." A variation of this activity is to have partners link right arms and circle for a count of four, then change direction for a second count of four.

Figure 8.8 Turns with a partner.

- The three-step turn, a popular basic turn in rhythmic gymnastics, requires direct teaching. Students initiate a sideways step, followed by a half turn of the body and a second step, followed by another half turn and a third (and final) step (figure 8.9).

- The push turn is a common jazz movement that can be used effectively in rhythmic gymnastics. Students walk forward on left then right feet. Take one more step and plant the left foot

Figure 8.9   Three-step turn.

firmly in front of the right. Students pivot to the right side by lifting up both heels, balancing on the both toes. Have students try another push turn using the right leg in front and pivoting to the left.

- Post colored or directional markings on the gym walls (e.g., red, blue, yellow, and green; N, S, E, and W). Call out a color or directional command and have students turn until they are facing the correct wall. If they are facing one direction and you call out that same direction (e.g., they are facing north and you call out, "North!"), then students have to perform a full rotation.

- From a standing position, students see if they can sit down gently into a crossed-legged sit by twisting their legs and lowering their bodies. For extra challenge, have them try rising to a standing position using the same movements performed in reverse.

- Students hold a balance on one foot and then try to rotate their bodies by shifting their weight on their standing (balance) foot. This type of rotation is initiated by lifting the heel and pivoting on the toe, then lifting the toe and pivoting on the heel. No hopping or jumping is allowed.

Summary

With thorough instruction in spatial awareness, students will deepen their understanding of the dimensions of space, in particular how their bodies can travel through these dimensions. A good understanding of spatial awareness early on will enable them to apply that knowledge in a safe manner later when they are given the opportunity to use hand apparatus. The addition of body elements, including balances, jumps, leaps, turns, pivots, and locomotion, will further enhance this understanding, laying the foundation for all the rhythmic gymnastics movements to come.

Chapter 9

© Helen Scott Studios

Rhythmic Gymnastics Skill Development

Now that the foundation for understanding spatial awareness has been developed, it is time to proceed to skill development using rhythmic gymnastics apparatus. This chapter discusses each of the fundamental elements for the ball, rope, hoop, ribbon, and scarf. A fundamental element is a movement that is basic to a specific piece of apparatus. For example, the predominant fundamental elements for the ball are bouncing, rolling, and throwing and catching and less dominant elements include swinging, circling, and figure 8s.

Each fundamental element discussion presents teaching tips to help you guide students' learning and assist them with skill development. Learning challenges, which are open-ended activities to help students discover what they can do with each apparatus, are also presented for each fundamental element. The learning challenges in this chapter are presented in a more abbreviated form than in chapter 8 for clarity and simplicity. Expand them or elaborate on them to suit the learning needs of your group of students.

Rhythmic Ball Skills

Rhythmic gymnastics ball skills and activities are varied and diverse. Before starting an introductory ball lesson, I ask students to name the sports that use balls and to list all of the different skills you can do using balls, like bouncing, throwing, and catching. Balls are a natural starting point for a rhythmic gymnastics unit because most students are familiar with them and they are fun to use.

When using rhythmic balls, try to connect instruction with other classroom learning whenever possible. For example, rhythmic bouncing patterns connect well to mathematical patterning in the early grades. The use of music will help to develop and promote musicality in students. And, through partner work and group routine building, students will further develop their teamwork and collaboration skills.

As with any rhythmic gymnastics apparatus, the ball should become a natural extension of the body and should be kept in fluid motion. Tell students to hold the ball with a cupped palm, rather than clutch it with their fingertips. There are other ways to grip a ball besides holding it in one hand, of course. The ball can be held with both hands, it can be maneuvered with the back of the hand, and it can be manipulated using different body parts (figure 9.1).

Ball skills can be divided into the following fundamental movement categories:

- Swing
- Circle
- Roll (on the body and the floor)
- Bounce
- Throw and catch
- Figure 8

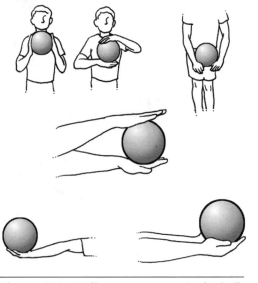

Figure 9.1   Different ways to grip the ball.

▶ Swings

A swing with a ball is a smooth motion similar to a pendulum. The ball can swing in one or two hands in a half arc. The movement is fluid and rhythmic.

Teaching Tips

- The ball should be balanced, not clutched, for one-handed swings; it should be held between the palms for two-handed swings.
- Stretch and bend the knees to help show a smooth rhythmic swing.
- A side swing is a progression for the one-handed throw.

Learning Challenges

- Swing the ball using one hand or both hands at the side or front of the body.
- Create a pattern using swings and circles (e.g., swing, swing, circle, swing). The circle is explained as the next fundamental element.
- Try a one-handed swing at the side of the body, then switch hands at the height of the swing. Try switching hands behind and in front of the body.
- Create a pattern using swings and bounces (figure 9.2; e.g., swing across the front of the body to the right, bounce, swing to the left, bounce).

Figure 9.2 Example of a swing and bounce combination.

▶ Circles

A circle is simply moving the ball in a circular pathway through space. The hands control the circle movement, usually in the frontal plane. Circles can be done with both hands holding the ball or with one hand using a change of grip.

Teaching Tips

- Circles are used as connecting moves.
- This basic skill usually requires that both hands be used or that the ball be passed from one hand to the other.

Learning Challenges

- Create as many different kinds of circles as possible using the ball. Circle the ball around different body parts (e.g., neck, waist, knees).
- With both hands on the ball, create a circle in front of the body. Use full arm extension to make the circle as big as possible.
- Create a front circle with the ball balanced in one hand (figure 9.3a). Try the same frontal circle, but this time move the ball in the left hand in a circle on the left side and move the ball in the right hand in a circle on the right side.
- Sitting in a V position, circle the ball under and then over the legs. Try another circle, this time moving the ball under the legs and behind the back (figure 9.3b).
- Try a backward arm circle to a small toss, then a forward arm circle to a bounce.

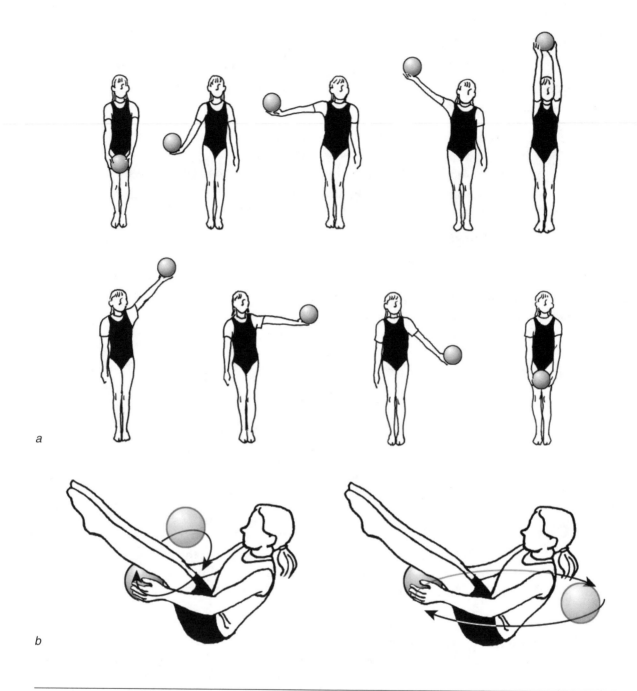

a

b

Figure 9.3 Circles with the ball *(a)* with the arm and *(b)* around the body.

▶ Rolls (on the Floor)

Rolling the ball on the floor is a gentle movement, requiring a gentle release of the ball to the floor. Allow the ball to roll off the fingertips onto the floor. While the ball rolls to the floor, students can perform body movements or travel to another space.

Teaching Tips

- Movement is soft and fluid.
- The ball stays in contact with the floor without bouncing.
- When released the ball rolls off the fingertips.

Learning Challenges

- Roll the ball on the floor following painted lines. Try rolling it without using the hands.
- Roll the ball over or on obstacles (e.g., benches, mats) as part of a ball circuit.
- Roll the ball in different pathways (e.g., straight, zigzag, curvy, wavy).
- Roll the ball from side to side while sitting cross-legged or in a V position, kneeling, standing, and so on (figure 9.4a).

a   b

Figure 9.4 Rolls on the floor.

- Roll the ball from front to back while sitting in an L position or kneeling (figure 9.4b).
- Roll the ball onto the floor, perform a gymnastics skill (e.g., side, back, or forward roll), and then retrieve the ball. (Be sure to use a mat.)
- Roll the ball on the floor in a slow roll, jump or leap over the ball, and then retrieve the ball.
- Lying facedown on the floor with arms stretched out to the sides, roll the ball from one hand to the other hand by lifting the torso and gently arching the back to allow the ball to pass under the upper torso. The head moves to watch the ball. The roll of the ball is initiated by a flick of the wrist (figure 9.5).
- Lying faceup, roll the ball under the body from side to side. (The hips must be raised to let the ball pass underneath; see figure 9.5.)
- Sitting on the floor, roll the ball from side to side under the legs. To increase the challenge, try rolling the ball from side to side while legs are raised in a V position.
- While standing, roll the ball on the floor in a figure 8 pattern around the legs.

Rolling under chest

Rolling under hips

Figure 9.5 Rolling ball under hips and chest.

- Lying facedown with arms stretched overhead, roll the ball lengthwise under the body while lifting and supporting the body in a push-up position. Stop the ball with the feet or ankles (figure 9.6).

Figure 9.6 Rolling ball under body.

▶ Body Roll

A body roll in rhythmic gymnastics can be either rolling the ball on a body part or rolling the body on the ball. The rolling movement should be smooth and fluid.

Teaching Tips

- The ball should remain in contact with the body to show a smooth and flowing roll.
- The pathway that the ball naturally follows is from the highest level to the lowest level.

Learning Challenges

- Sitting with the legs straight out, push the ball to roll it up and down the legs (figure 9.7). Then try to roll the ball up and down the legs without using the hands (i.e., raise and lower the legs).

- Begin by holding the ball using both hands with the arms straight in front of the body. Initiate an arm roll by gently raising the arms. Let the ball roll down the arms to the chin, then lower the arms to roll the ball back to the hands (see figure 9.7).

Figure 9.7   Body rolls on the legs and arms.

- Holding the ball at the back of the neck, gently release the ball and allow it to roll down the back. Change hand position to catch the ball at the lower back.
- Roll the ball up one arm, from the hand to the shoulder, and then continue rolling the ball down the back, catching it at the lower back (figure 9.8).
- The goal of these activities is to progress to a full arm roll where the ball rolls across outstretched arms from one hand to the other. Begin by rolling the ball up and down one arm with the free hand assisting the roll. Try this on both the right and left arms. Then try to roll the ball across two outstretched arms using the free hand to assist the roll (i.e., the left hand helps the roll on the right arm and the right arm helps the roll on the left arm). Finally, try the roll across the entire arm span—beginning in one hand travelling up the entire arm, across the upper chest and down the second arm to rest in the second hand. Initiate the roll by slightly raising the hand and stretching the palm open to start a gentle roll.

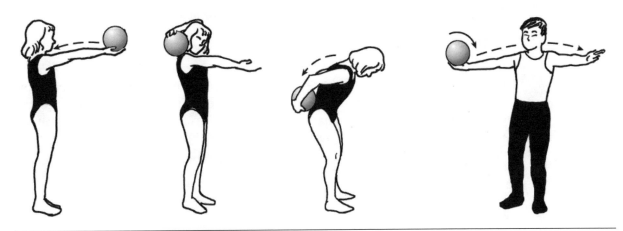

Figure 9.8   Rolls on the body.

- Kneeling with the ball on the floor in front of the body, initiate a body roll by placing the hands on the floor and letting the chest roll forward on top of the ball. At the end of the movement, the arms straighten, the back arches slightly (with the lower torso still on the floor), and the ball stays trapped between the body and the floor (figure 9.9). Reverse the movement to return to the original starting position.

Figure 9.9   Roll on the ball.

▶ Bounces

Bouncing is a skill familiar to nearly all children. Rhythmic gymnastics bouncing emphasizes rhythmic patterns, control, and a specific motion of pushing the ball to the floor. Posture is important in bounces. The head and body should stay tall and straight while the hands initiate the bounce.

Teaching Tips

- Press the ball to the floor with a rounded and stable wrist.
- Round the fingers and palm to conform to the shape of the ball.
- The hand should stay in contact with the ball for as long as possible.

Learning Challenges

- Bounce the ball at different levels. Create a pattern that clearly shows the transition from a high bounce to a low or medium bounce (e.g., 2 high bounces, 2 low bounces, 2 medium bounces, 1 high bounce, catch). Try the same challenge, but this time the body should mimic the levels. For example, sit for a low bounce, kneel for a medium bounce, and stand for a high bounce.
- Show how the ball can be bounced using different body parts (e.g., elbows, chest, head, back of hand, toes).
- Create a bouncing pattern with a change of tempo (e.g., three quick, short bounces followed by three slow, tall bounces).
- Bounce the ball while traveling using various types of locomotion (e.g., skipping, running, walking, sliding, galloping).

- While sitting on the floor in a straddle position, bounce the ball in front then close the legs and bounce the ball to the side. Continue this pattern and try to increase the tempo of the leg switches and the bounces (figure 9.10).
- Let the ball travel in a V shape by bouncing it from one hand to the other. After mastering the V bounce, try bouncing the ball under a lifted leg (figure 9.10).

Figure 9.10 Bouncing variations: Bouncing in a straddle with a change to an L sit and a V bounce.

- From the front side of the body, bounce the ball between the legs and catch it behind.
- Starting on one side, bounce the ball behind the back, then twist the body around to the other side and catch the ball (figure 9.11).

▶ Throws and Catches

Throwing and catching are fundamental motor skills essential to children's physical development. When introducing throws and catches emphasize that the ball should remain in control

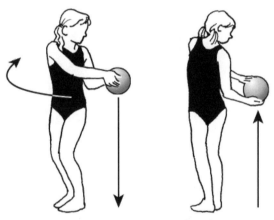

Figure 9.11 Bounce ball behind back, turn 360°, and catch.

at all times. For a quiet, controlled catch, the ball should be absorbed with the hands and the entire body.

Teaching Tips

- The ball should roll off the end of the hand, passing over the fingertips on release.
- Use the entire arm, stretching and extending in the direction of the throw.
- Keep the knees flexed during a catch and extended during a throw.
- For a quiet catch, absorb the ball so that it rolls gently into the palm.
- Control the ball at all times. Students have a tendency to throw the ball very high and are then unable to catch it successfully.
- Opportunities for repetition and practice are recommended.

Learning Challenges

- Introductory throwing and catching activities allow students to practice throwing the ball at a level where they can then successfully catch it. Try throwing from one hand or both hands, or alternate between the left and right hand.
- Throw the ball and allow it to bounce before catching it. Throw the ball and perform a task or movement before catching the ball. The following sequences are some examples:
  - Throw the ball, touch the floor, then catch the ball.
  - Throw the ball, clap as many times as possible, then catch the ball.
  - Throw the ball into the air, perform a full turn, then catch the ball.
- Throw and catch the ball from different levels (e.g., throw from a low level and catch at a high level).
- Throw and catch the ball using different body parts (e.g., throw with one hand and catch between the elbows, throw with both hands and catch between the knees while sitting with knees pointing up on the floor).
- With the right hand, throw the ball under the left arm and then catch it in the left hand. Switch sides (figure 9.12).
- Throw the ball straight up overhead, move the torso a few degrees forward, and catch the ball at the lower back (figure 9.12).

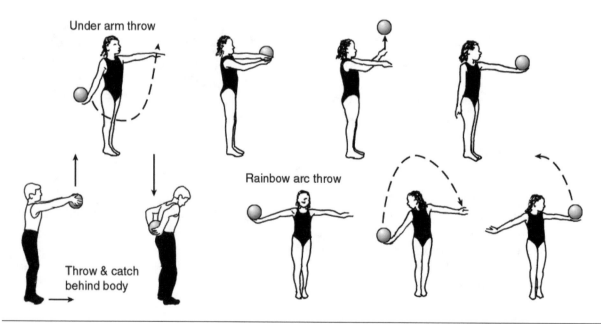

Figure 9.12 Various throws: throw under arm and catch; throw from the front and catch in the back; rainbow toss from side to side.

- Throw the ball with one hand in a rainbow arc (i.e., overhead) and catch it with the opposite hand (figure 9.12).
- In a sitting position, hold the ball between the feet and try to throw it using only the feet.

▶ Figure 8s

Figure 8s are a more complex skill with the ball. Thus, this element may be most suitable for older students.

Teaching Tips

- The figure 8 pattern can be created on the floor, horizontally or vertically.
- The figure 8 pattern can be done with one hand or both hands holding the ball.

Learning Challenges

- Create the figure 8 pattern on the floor by rolling the ball around one foot and then around the other.
- With both hands holding the ball, create a horizontal figure 8 pattern (i.e., on its side) and a vertical figure 8 pattern (i.e., standing upright). Figure 9.13 shows examples of both of these.
- Demonstrate the advanced skill of a horizontal figure 8 by breaking it down into two phases. Begin by holding the ball to the

Figure 9.13 Figure 8s with the ball in the frontal plane.

side. Then move the ball inward toward the body, by bringing it under the arm. Continue this pathway until the arm is stretched straight and to the side. Then perform the second phase where the arm travels in a circular path and returns to the starting position (figure 9.14).

Finish in same pose as #1

Figure 9.14 Horizontal figure 8 with a ball—back view.

▶ Partner and Group Work

There are many opportunities to develop group work skills using the ball. Throwing, rolling, and bouncing are more fun when done with a partner. Incorporate group activities into your lessons as often as possible to give students the experience of working with others on a common task.

Teaching Tips

- Have students communicate with their partners and discuss what each person will do.
- Switch tasks so that every student has a chance to try each skill.
- Try to keep the ball in control at all times.

Learning Challenges

- Demonstrate the ways to roll the ball to a partner. Use one ball, then two balls.
- Show an exchange (i.e., one student throws and the other rolls the ball). Invent another exchange using rolls and throws.
- Invent an exchange where one partner faces backward and is unable to see where the ball is going.
- Roll the ball down both outstretched arms, off the end of the fingertips, into the hands of a partner (figure 9.15).

Figure 9.15   Rolling a ball on the arms between partners.

Rope Skills

The rope is a dynamic and versatile rhythmic gymnastics apparatus, and most children will be familiar with it. The intricacies and variety of skills involved make the rope an interesting piece of equipment to work with. The rope can be used to develop cardiovascular fitness through skipping and jumping activities. Various rope skills, including manipulation as well as release and catch, can improve hand-eye coordination. For example, the rope can be thrown in a controlled manner into the air, or one end of the rope can be released and then caught. The rope can wrap and unwrap around body parts in simple or intricate ways. And the rope can swing or rotate in all three planes and at different speeds. Finally, the total body coordination needed for rope skipping makes it an excellent tool for developing the overall body.

Use of music with a good tempo and an audible beat will help children develop a skipping rhythm. As students' skill levels increase you can choose music with a faster tempo. For safety, ensure that students have ample area to rotate the rope freely and that they are jumping on a smooth, flat surface. When doing a large amount of skipping, it is important for children to wear suitable athletic footwear that will absorb the shock of the jumping action.

As explained in chapter 2, plastic skipping ropes are not appropriate for rhythmic gymnastics. The rope should be flexible and pliable. Likewise, the rope should not have handles, although knots can be tied on the ends for easier gripping and catching. Thicker and braided ropes will be easier for young students to see and control.

There are several ways to grip the rope in rhythmic gymnastics, aside from the traditional skipping grasp of the hands placed on the ends of the rope. The rope can be held at middle points; divided into quarters, thirds, and halves; and held in one hand or both hands (figure 9.16). Different grips allow for interesting variations of several skills.

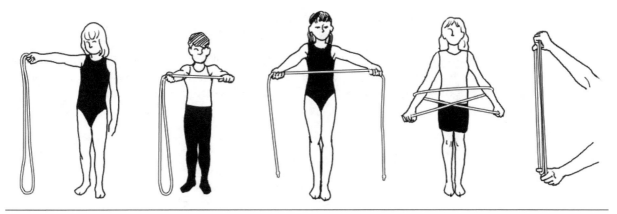

Figure 9.16 Various ways to grip the rope.

Fundamental elements for the rope are in many ways similar to the basic elements of other equipment, such as swings and throws and catches. There are also elements that are very specific and exclusive to rope such as releasing, wrapping and jumping and skipping. The most familiar fundamental element to rope is of course jumping and skipping. The fundamental movements for rope are the following:

- Swing
- Jump and skip
- Rotate
- Wrap
- Release
- Throw and catch

▶ Swings

A swing with the rope is a gentle pendulum motion. The hand and arm initiate the movement and control the speed of the swing. When done with the rope folded in half, swings are the preparation for a rotation.

Teaching Tips

- Swinging elements with the rope should be smooth and fluid motions.
- The hands and arms should follow the swinging movement of the rope to help the rope maintain a uniform U shape.
- The rope can be held using various grips—for example, both ends in one hand, an end in each hand, and the middle section in both hands.

Learning Challenges

- Swing the rope in front of the body. Try gripping the rope with one hand on each end. Keep the rope in a nice U shape. Try to keep the swing going while putting both ends of the rope in one hand.
- This basic swing is called an underarm swing. Swing the rope at the side of the body, forward and then backward with one end of the rope in each hand. Switch sides and swing the rope on the other side of the body. Try the same movement with the rope folded in half and held by one hand. Switch the rope from one hand to the other when changing sides.

- Swing the rope to the beat of a smooth, flowing piece of music. When the music stops, the body stops, in a frozen statue. See what the rope will do.
- Swing the rope in front of the body (frontal plane). Then, without affecting the swing, move the body a quarter turn so the rope is swinging at the side of the body (side swing). This is a transition from a frontal plane swing to a side swing (figure 9.17).

Figure 9.17 Swing in front plane with quarter turn to side plane swing.

- While swinging the rope, add some locomotion movements (e.g., walking, waltzing, tiptoeing).
- Try a swing that starts out very slow. Increase the speed of the swing and turn the swing into a rotation. Then slow down the rotation and change back to a swinging motion.
- Swing the rope forward in front of the body and, as the rope swings back, jump over it. As it swings forward, jump over it again. Try the same type of jump, but this time jump sideways as the rope swings from side to side.

▶ Partner and Group Work

- With a partner, find a way to swing two ropes at the same time. Do it again, but this time with each partner holding one end of both ropes.
- Partners hold a rope between them and swing the rope. A third student jumps over the rope as it swings. Change roles so that everyone gets to jump.

▶ Jumps and Skips

Rope jumping and skipping are excellent for the development of fitness and overall coordination. Rope jumping can be modified in intensity and duration to suit the fitness levels of participants. Difficulty can be increased by linking skills together and by increasing the speed at which the skills are performed. The learning challenges are arranged to provide ideas for pre-skipping before adding activities for those children who have mastered basic jump rope skipping.

Teaching Tips

- When jumping, land lightly on the balls of the feet and touch the heels quickly to the floor.

- The upper body should remain upright with good posture, making the jumping activity appear effortless.
- The legs and feet should remain close together. For speed skipping, jumps are small and close to the ground. For slower jumping, the toes stretch downward and the legs are fully extended when in the air.
- Emphasize an even tempo and rhythm when skipping.
- The hands and wrists should rotate at the sides of the body, near the hips.

Learning Challenges

Some children will master these basic skills easily, while others will need more practice. Non-skippers should begin with the pre-skipping activities; proficient skippers can progress to the more advanced skipping and jumping skills.

Pre-skipping activities

- Fold the rope in half and stretch it out in front of the body holding it with both hands. Step over the rope with both feet and pass the rope behind the back all the way to the front of your body again. Now try to do the same thing but with the rope folded into thirds. Try it with the rope folded into quarters. This activity improves shoulder flexibility by decreasing the distance between the hands with each change in the rope's size.

Note: All of the following activities use a rope stretched out on the floor.

- Jump over the rope as many times as possible within the time allotted.
- Jump back and forth across the rope from one end to the other. Try to zigzag backward down the rope.
- On one foot hop back and forth along the length of the rope. Change feet and return to the other end.
- Walk on the rope as if it is a tightrope. Walk forward, backward, and sideways. Try using a crossstep. Use the hands and arms to balance.
- Keeping both hands on the floor (one hand on each side of the rope), jump back and forth across the rope.
- Jump over the "stream." Stretch out two ropes parallel. Try to jump over both ropes. Gradually increase the distance between the ropes for more challenge.

▶ Partner and Group Work

- Two partners stand on the rope, like it is a tightrope. Then one partner tries to pass the other partner without falling off.
- Partners stretch a long rope between them and wiggle the rope (like a snake) on the ground. A third person tries to jump over the "snake" without touching it. Switch roles so that each student gets to be the jumper.
- Partners stretch one rope between them. One partner holds it low to the ground. The other holds it waist

Figure 9.18 Jumping over a stretched rope.

high. Teach the figure 8 patterns of traveling around each rope ender and jumping over the rope at the level/height that is most comfortable (figure 9.18).

Advanced skipping and jumping skills—traditional skipping with rope end held in each hand

- Jump forward, backward, and sideways using different styles and variations (e.g., both feet, alternating feet, high stepping, kicking toes to the front, kicking heels to the back, and so on).

- Crossovers are popular skipping skills. While skipping, cross the arms in front and jump through the loop made by the rope. After the rope passes under the feet and behind the back open the arms and skip through the rope.

- Rotate the rope twice to each jump (i.e., the rope will pass under the feet twice for every jump.

- Create different jumping patterns (e.g., 4 jumps on 2 feet followed by 2 jumps on the left foot and then 2 jumps on the right foot).

- Hold one end of the rope in each hand. Rotate the rope on each side of body, and when rope is overhead open the arms and then jump over the open rope (figure 9.19). Repeat the pattern. Then create combinations of rotations and jumps (e.g., rotate on the left, open up the rope and jump with both feet, then rotate on the right).

- Create jumping patterns using different foot positions (e.g., jump side to side like a down hill skier; jump with the feet apart on one jump and together on the next jump; twist the lower body one way on one jump and the other way on the next jump; cross the feet on one jump and then uncross them on the second jump).

- Perform the jump, half turn, backward jump (figure 9.20). (This skill is advanced and will require direct teaching.) Jump over the rope with both feet. As the rope comes overhead the body turns 180 degrees, making the rope come together and rotate at the left side of the body. Open the rope and jump backward over the rope. For extra challenge, try moving from the backward jump to a forward jump with a half turn. Jump backward over the rope, then let the rope come together as the body turns 180 degrees and jump over the rope facing forward.

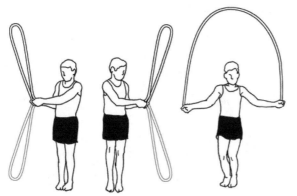

Figure 9.19   Side figure 8 with jump through rope.

Figure 9.20 Jump through rope, half turn with a swing, back jump through rope.

▶ Partner and Group Work

- Two students stand side by side with a rope end in each hand and the rope behind resting on the floor. The hands that are closest to each other exchange rope ends. Now try to turn the rope and jump together (figure 9.21).
- Try the same type of skipping in a group of three.
- Try some of the other group and partner skipping shown in figure 9.21.

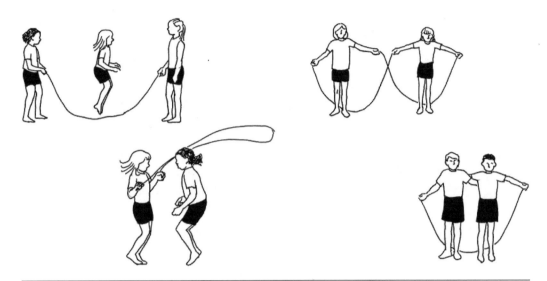

Figure 9.21   Rope jumping skills with a partner or group of three.

▶ Rotations

A basic rope rotation is performed by holding the two ends of a folded rope in one hand. The wrist initiates and sustains the rotation. To sustain the plane of the rope, rotations must be done quickly. Rotations can be clockwise or counterclockwise in the frontal plane, forward and backward in the side plane, and overhead in the horizontal plane. A rotation at the side of the body followed by a rotation on the other side of the body creates a figure 8 pattern.

Teaching Tips

- Rope rotations can be simply described as spinning the rope like the blade of a helicopter.
- Rotations can be performed at the front and sides of the body as well as overhead. They can also be performed parallel to the floor.
- The rotating action comes primarily from the wrist. The momentum of the rope keeps the rotation going.
- Rotations are preparations for throws.

Figure 9.22 Rotations with the rope in three planes: front, side, and horizontal.

Learning Challenges

- Fold the rope in half and rotate it in different planes as in figure 9.22 (e.g., in front of the body [frontal], at the sides of the body [sagittal], and overhead [horizontal]).

- Rotate the rope on one side of the body and then on the other (i.e., making a figure 8).

- Rotate the rope so that it is parallel to and just skimming the floor. Jump over the rope as it approaches the feet. Try different styles of jumps (e.g., two foot, step over, one foot jump).

- Grasp the middle of the rope with both hands. Rotate the ends of the rope forward and backward. Then try to alternate the rotation (i.e., right rotates followed by left in rapid sucession, similar to the rope motion of double dutch).

- Grip the rope at its end and midpoint and try various rotations (e.g., overhead, frontal, sagittal) using this half rope length.

- Rotate the rope overhead and change levels while maintaining the rotation (figure 9.23).

- Rotate the rope and show a body turn, a jump, or a leap.

Figure 9.23 Rotations overhead with change of level.

▶ Wraps

Rope wrapping is when the rope is wound and then unwound around various parts of the body. The rope can wrap around the knees, waist, ankles, and arms. It can be wrapped when folded or full length, and in a closed (i.e., both ends in one hand) or open (i.e., one end in each hand) position.

Teaching Tips

- Wrapping the rope around the body is a way to show the versatility of the rope beyond the more familiar elements such as jumping and skipping. The rope can be wrapped in various ways (e.g., folded rope or open rope) and in various places on the body.

- Use soft, braided ropes for rhythmic gymnastics rope activities; beaded or speed-skipping ropes are not suitable.

- Never wrap the rope around the neck.

Learning Challenges

- Stretch the rope on the floor in a straight line, holding one end, and roll the body like a log on the floor to make the rope wrap around the waist. Roll back the other way to make the rope unwrap.

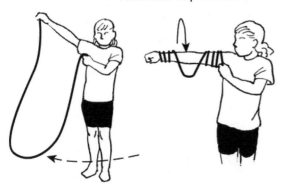

- With the rope folded in half, or with one end in each hand, wrap it around the waist. In a larger space, holding one end of the rope, rotate the rope in its full length then wrap around the body starting at the waist. The rotation will have to be strong and powerful enough to gain the momentum to wrap the body.

- Try to wrap different body parts with the rope (e.g., wrap the wrists, ankles, and knees).

- Using an underarm swing, wrap the rope around one arm outstretched to the side (figure 9.24). Then try to unwrap it. Try unwrapping with locomotion.

Figure 9.24 Arm wrap from a swing.

▶ Releases, Throws, and Catches

In rhythmic gymnastics a release movement is when one end of the rope is released while the other end of the rope is held. A throw is when the entire rope is released at the same time. Catches are usually done by grasping the ends of the rope but can also be performed by catching the middle section of the rope. Releases are a great place to start because students have more control when releasing than when trying a full throw. Throwing and catching are more challenging skills and, therefore, more suitable for older students.

Teaching Tips

- These skills are fairly technical and will likely require direct teaching.
- The challenge in throwing, catching, and releasing is combining these skills with other movements.

Learning Challenges

- Walk the dog (figure 9.25). (I like to teach this release movement first. Children as young as five or six can master this skill with practice.) Stretch out the rope

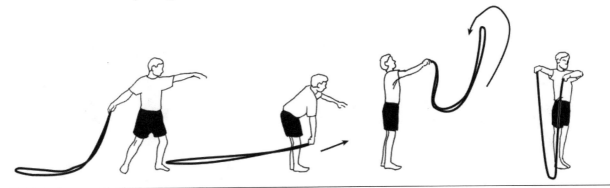

Figure 9.25 Walk the dog, release, and catch.

behind the body on the floor, keeping one end of the rope in one hand (as if leading a dog on a leash—hence the name of this activity). Take two or three steps forward and pull the rope forward. Catch the free end, which will fly outward and upward when pulled, with the free hand.

- Swing the rope in front of the body with one hand on each end, maintaining a uniform U shape during the swing. When swinging to the right, release the left end of the rope and let it fly to the right. With the right hand drag the rope back along the floor in front of you to the to the right side. The free end will fly into the air and can be caught by the left hand (figure 9.26). For extra challenge, try catching the free end in the hand that is already holding the other rope end (in this case, the right hand).

Figure 9.26   Release of rope from a front swing, pull, and regrasp.

- Try some of the other group and partner skipping shown in Figure 9.21.
- With one end of the rope in each hand, swing the rope at the side of the body in an underarm swing. When swinging forward, release the ends and grasp the rope in the middle section with the rope ends trailing down. Continue by rotating the rope ends.
- Skipping the rope backward, when the rope passes under the feet, throw it upward into the air. Try to catch the falling rope in front of you (figure 9.27a).
- From a rotation at the side of the body, throw the rope into the air and catch it (figure 9.27b).

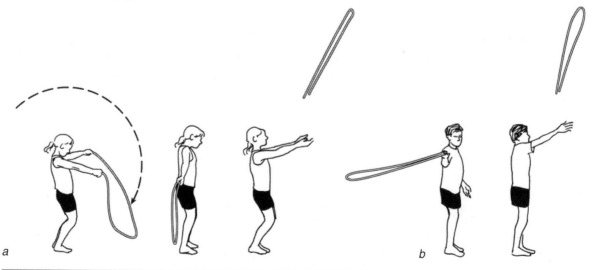

a   *b*

Figure 9.27   Throws with the rope: *(a)* backward skip and *(b)* from side rotation.

Hoop Skills

Hoops are found in almost every school's equipment room. Hoops are also readily available from physical education supply stores and rhythmic gymnastics supply companies, or you can make your own (see chapter 2). If hoops are too heavy they are hard to manipulate in the correct planes. If too light, they are also difficult to manipulate, although extra weight can be added by wrapping them with tape. Before using the hoop in your rhythmic gymnastics unit, check to make sure that there are no rough spots or protruding staples that may scratch or cut students.

When you first give students a hoop, their natural inclination will be to "hula hoop" (i.e., rotate the hoop around their hips), but there are many other skills and tricks that can be mastered. Rhythmic gymnastics hoop elements can be divided into the following categories:

- Swing
- Circle
- Roll
- Spin
- Throw and catch
- Rotation
- Pass (through or over the hoop)

There are various ways to grip a hoop (figure 9.28). The grip should be light, but firm enough to maintain control. There are five basic grips: overhand, underhand, mixed, fingertip, and bird perch.

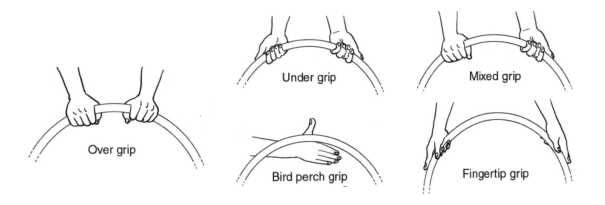

Figure 9.28   Grips on the hoop.

▶ Swings

A hoop swing is similar to swings with the rope and ball. A swing is a pendulum motion that resembles a half circle. Swings can be performed in the frontal and sagittal (side) planes. In frontal swings the hoop is usually held with both hands; in sagittal swings the hoop is usually held with one hand.

Teaching Tips

- Grip the hoop lightly.
- Swings should not hit the ground but should lightly skim the surface.
- Swings are relaxed and natural, rhythmic movements, not stiff or frenetic.
- Sagittal swings are good preparation for throws and catches, rotations, and boomerang rolls.

Learning Challenges

- Using a one- or two-handed overhand grip, swing the hoop in front of the body.
- Swing the hoop at the side of the body, first with one hand and then with the other using an overhand grip.
- Try switching hands in front of the body at the height of the side swing, then behind the back at the back of the swing.
- At the very top of a side swing, stop the momentum of the hoop and hold it and the body in a balance position. Continue with the swing to the opposite side of the body.
- Try the "picture frame" swing (figure 9.29). Start by holding the hoop in front of you with a two-handed underhand grip. While still holding on with the underhand grip, flip the hoop up so that it is in front of the face (like a round picture frame). Then let the hoop swing in front and then swing out away from the body. Return to the picture frame position. Repeat the swing on the other side of the body. Eventually, when the skill is mastered, the swing can become a fluid motion that is very visually exciting that looks more difficult than it really is to perform.

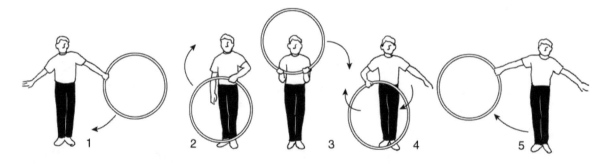

Figure 9.29   Picture frame swing.

- Try a swing behind the body similar to the picture frame swing (figure 9.30). (Swinging the hoop at the back of the body is technical and will likely require direct teaching.) Hold the hoop out to the side of the body using an underhand grip. Swing the hoop behind the back and grasp it with the other hand (with the insides of the wrist facing outwards). Continue the swing back to the other side.

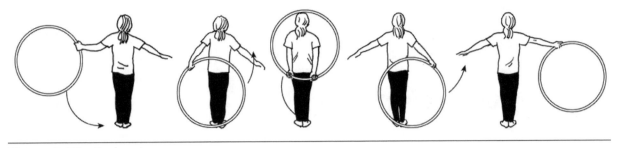

Figure 9.30   Back swing.

Partner and Group Work

- Partners stand facing each other. Each person swings the hoop using the same hand (figure 9.31). After a few practice swings, partners exchange hoops at the top of the swing. You will be giving away a hoop from one hand while receiving your partner's hoop with the other hand.

Figure 9.31   Side swings with a partner.

▶ Circles

There are two types of circles using the hoop. A circle in the frontal plane requires a change of hands and grip as the hoop passes overhead and then in front of the body. A circle in the horizontal plane also requires a change of grip as the hoop passes around the body.

Teaching Tips

- Circles with the hoop require a change of hands and grip.
- Circles are less common than the other fundamental hoop elements.

Learning Challenges

- Using an overhand grip and sitting cross legged or kneeling, pass the hoop around the body, lightly skimming the floor (figure 9.32a). After mastering this skill, slowly rise from the floor and try to keep circling the hoop around the body at different levels (e.g., ankles, knees, hips, or in a V sit position; figure 9.32b).

Figure 9.32   Circling hoop around body *(a)* from kneeling position; *(b)* from V sit.

- Begin this circle by holding the hoop in front of you using an underhand grip. Circle the hoop by extending it out to the side, then overhead (change hands), back down the other side to the starting position (figure 9.33).

Figure 9.33   Circle in the front plane with change of hands.

▶ Rolls

In rhythmic gymnastics, the hoop is rolled on the floor. This is a basic and fun skill for children. To add challenge, encourage students to try different body movements while the hoop is rolling, such as skipping alongside the hoop.

Teaching Tips

- Rolls should be smooth. The hoop should maintain contact with the floor throughout the roll.
- Rolls can be initiated with the hand on top of the hoop, pressing down and forward, or with the hand on the side of the hoop, pushing it forward.
- Always maintain control of the hoop and look forward when traveling with the hoop.

Learning Challenges

- Roll the hoop on the floor into an open space, then run and catch it. Try using both the right and the left hand to initiate the roll.
- After rolling the hoop, run ahead of the hoop and let it roll into the hand.
- Roll the hoop and then run alongside it to keep it rolling.
- Roll the hoop from side to side in a lunge position. Shift and stretch the body to lengthen the roll (figure 9.34).
- Perform a boomerang roll, which is a forward roll with a backspin (figure 9.35). (When rolled with the boomerang technique, the hoop rolls a certain distance and then comes back—hence the name of the roll.) Use a small swing to bring the hoop backward at the side of the body. As the hoop is brought forward in the swing, put a small backspin on the hoop before releasing it forward to roll on the floor. The boomerang is an advanced skill that is quite versatile once mastered. Try the following skills in combination with a boomerang.

- When the hoop returns jump over it, or let it pass under one leg and catch it behind the back.
- Perform a sequence of three or four body elements before the hoop returns (e.g., touch the floor, jump, turn around, balance, and then catch it).
- As it returns, stop the hoop by trapping it with the foot or hand.
- Catch the hoop as it returns between your knees by clamping your legs together.

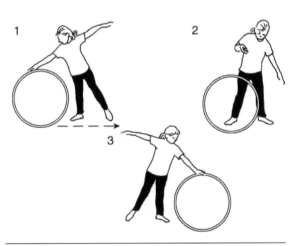

Figure 9.34   Rolling hoop in front of body.

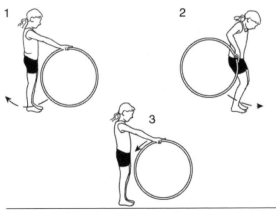

Figure 9.35   Boomerang roll.

Partner and Group Work

- Roll a hoop to a partner. Add more challenge by moving farther apart.
- Partners roll two hoops, trying to release the hoops at the same time.
- One partner rolls the hoop, the other tries to go through the hoop without interrupting the roll.
- Three students stand in a triangle formation, each holding a hoop. Each student simultaneously rolls a hoop to the next person (following a clockwise or counterclockwise direction). Immediately after rolling the hoop, students must quickly look for and try to catch the hoop rolling toward them (figure 9.36a).
- In a group of three, two students roll the hoop between them. The third student tries to jump over the hoop (figure 9.36b).

Figure 9.36   Group of three *(a)* rolling the hoop in a triangle formation, *(b)* partner roll with third person jumping over rolling hoop.

▶ Spins

A hoop spin is the rotation of the hoop around its vertical axis. A spin is an easy skill to perform, yet visually exciting to watch. For more challenge, encourage students to explore what they can do with their bodies while the hoop is spinning.

Teaching Tips

- Spins usually occur on the floor.

- To initiate the spin, grasp the hoop and then twist and flick it with the wrist.

Learning Challenges

Figure 9.37   Traveling around the spinning hoop.

- Spin the hoop on the floor. Try using both the right and the left hand to initiate the spin. Also try to spin it in both clockwise and counterclockwise directions. When the spin slows down, catch the hoop.
- Initiate a spin, then run and touch a wall, returning to catch the hoop before it drops.
- Spin the hoop, then travel around using different movements while it's spinning (figure 9.37). Try skipping, running, or side galloping around the spinning hoop.
- Spin the hoop, wait for it to slow down, then jump into the hoop.
- After a spin show and hold a balance for 3 seconds, followed by a second balance of 3 seconds. Then catch the hoop.
- Spin the hoop, then pass a body part over the hoop combined with a turn.

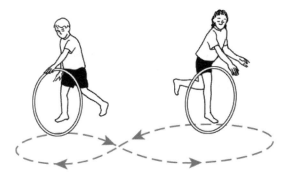

Figure 9.38 Partner work with spins.

Partner and Group Work

- Partners spin their own hoops and then trade places to catch their partner's hoop. Add a movement while passing each other (e.g., clap, jump three times, turn around, clap, and then catch the hoop).

- Partners spin their own hoops and then run in a figure 8 pattern around the spinning hoops, completing the pattern before the hoops fall to the floor (figure 9.38). (Students will need to discuss which way they will travel before beginning this activity.)

▶ Throws and Catches

Throwing and catching a hoop is a challenging skill, one best reserved for older students. A hoop throw can be performed in the horizontal plane (like a flipping pancake), from a rotation on the hand, or from a side swing. Catches can be performed with one or both hands.

Teaching Tips

- Watch the hoop carefully to ensure a successful catch.
- Try a small throw (or toss) before a large throw.
- In the horizontal plane, try throwing the hoop with only one rotation before trying a larger throw where the hoop rotates several times.

Learning Challenges

- Try various combinations of throws and catches using both right and left hands (e.g., throw from a side swing using one hand and catch it with both hands, throw with one hand and catch in the other hand).

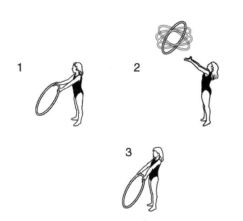

Figure 9.39 Pancake toss with the hoop—catch in both hands.

- Throw and catch the hoop from a side swing while traveling forward, backward, or sideways.
- From a side swing, gently toss the hoop into the air and catch it. Try to catch the hoop before it hits the floor. If the hoop bounces, it should bounce toward, not away from, the body.
- Throw the hoop, hold a balance, and then catch the hoop. Then throw the hoop and perform a body movement (e.g., clap the hands, turn or pivot, jump) before catching the hoop.
- Perform a "pancake toss," flipping the hoop in the air as if flipping a pancake. The hoop should rotate one to three times before being caught (figure 9.39).

Figure 9.40   Pizza toss—hoop remains horizontal in the air and does not rotate.

- Perform a "pizza toss." Hold the hoop horizontally in front of the body. Throw the hoop up by bending the knees and then pushing the hoop into the air. The "pizza" should remain flat so that the "toppings" do not fall off. Catch the hoop with one or two hands (figure 9.40).

- While performing a high "pizza toss," try to get under the hoop so that it drops down around the body like a ring going over a peg. For extra challenge, try to catch the hoop before it hits the ground.

- Add other skills to the "pizza toss" (e.g., throw the hoop in a "pizza toss" movement, then grab it in the air and skip through it).

Partner and Group Work

- Partners face each other and, from a side swing, throw the hoop gently to each other. Try the same activity, but this time partners stand side by side and throw the hoop up in the air. The student on the left will throw the hoop with his right hand and the one on the right will catch it with her left hand. Create more partner exchanges.

- Create exchange patterns using rolls and catches (e.g., throw, throw, roll, roll, and repeat).

▶ Rotations

In a hoop rotation the hoop rotates around an axis, usually a hand or an arm. Usually rotating around the wrist is not comfortable, as the wrist is too bony. When learning this skill, students may want to try rotating the hoop on the forearm. For proper technique, students should be encouraged to try rotating the hoop in the webbed part of the hand (i.e., between the thumb and index finger).

Teaching Tips

- The bird perch grip is used for hoop rotations on the hand.

- Hoop rotations are usually around a body part that serves as the axis (e.g., hand, torso, waist).

- Rotations can be performed in all three planes. Maintaining an exact plane during the rotation is challenging for most students.

Learning Challenges

- Rotate around any body part (arm, knees, hand, waist; figure 9.41).

- Rotating the hoop around the waist, travel across the floor. Try a walk, gallop, sliding step, or crossover step. Try to keep the hoop action going.

Figure 9.41 Rotations around different body parts.

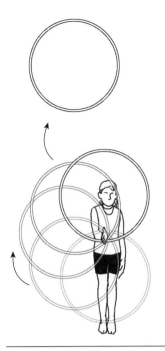

Figure 9.42 Throw from a rotation.

- Rotate the hoop around a hand or arm (figure 9.42). Initiate the rotation with a gentle swing of the hoop. Try this rotation clockwise and counterclockwise, and in front of the body and at the side.
- Rotate the hoop on one hand overhead. Keep the rotation going and turn the body a full turn. Try other movements while rotating the hoop overhead.
- Rotate the hoop overhead and let the hoop travel down the body while maintaining the rotation.
- While rotating the hoop on one hand in the frontal plane, try to switch hands while keeping the rotation going.
- From a rotation in front of the body, throw the hoop upward. Try the same throw from a side rotation. For more challenge, catch the hoop using the bird perch grip and continue the rotation.

Partner and Group Work

- In groups of two, designate a learner and a leader. The leader will help the learner feel the rotation motion. The learner places one hand between the leader's hands inside the hoop (figure 9.43a). The leader initiates the rotation movement, then gently and slowly removes her hands so that the learner is rotating the hoop on his own.
- Resting a hoop on the wrists, partners grasp hands (as if shaking hands; figure 9.43b). Working together, try to rotate the hoop without letting go of each other's hands.

a   b

Figure 9.43 Helping a partner learn how to rotate a hoop. *(a)* Learner's hand is between both of leader's. *(b)* Rotating hoops together with clasped hands.

▶ Passing Over or Through the Hoop

Passing over or through the hoop includes a variety of skills and movements in rhythmic gymnastics, each of which show diversity in how the body interacts with the action of the hoop. The most familiar skills in this category are skipping through the hoop or jumping over a hoop. Students' creativity and imaginations will lead them to create many other innovative skills.

Teaching Tips

- Passing through or over the hoop includes any action in which the body moves partway in and then out of a hoop, or all the way through a hoop.
- The body, or parts of the body, can also pass over the hoop.

Learning Challenges

- Lay hoops out on the floor. With music playing in the background, lift up and pass through as many hoops as possible in the time allowed.
- Lay hoops out in a pathway (e.g., serpent, zigzag) and travel along the pathway using specific movements (e.g., hopping on one foot, jumping, and so on).
- With hoops flat on the floor, practice jumping in various ways (e.g., jump forward into the hoop, jump backward out of the hoop, jump sideways in and out of the hoop).

- With hoops flat on the floor, put both hands in the hoop and let the feet walk around its perimeter. Reverse the movement, keeping both feet in the hoop and move the hands around the outside perimeter.
- Jump in and out of the hoop, traveling around the edge until back at the starting position.
- Hop on one foot all the way around the outside of the hoop, then switch feet and hop all the way around in the other direction.
- Roll the hoop on the floor and, maintaining the roll, pass through it.
- Hold the hoop overhead horizontally. Let the hoop drop to the ground without touching any part of the body (figure 9.44). For a variation, try catching the hoop before it hits the ground.
- Holding the hoop with one hand or both hands, skip through the hoop (figure 9.45). Try it forward, backward, and even sideways. Jump with both feet, alternate feet, or other skipping variations. Try skipping backward.
- Cartwheel over a hoop lying flat on the floor, and try to pick up the hoop while passing over it.

Figure 9.44 Cylinder—keep hoop horizontal to floor.

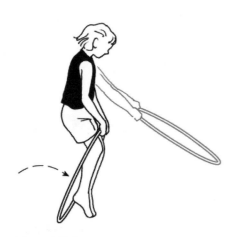

Figure 9.45 Skipping through the hoop—hands use over grip.

Partner and Group Work

- Perform a "thread the needle" (figure 9.46a). Students line up holding hands (about 5 to 10 students per line). The student at the end of the human chain holds a hoop out to the side. The student at the end of the line gently pulls the human chain through the hoop. The student holding the hoop will be the last one to pass through it. Repeat the process in reverse by having students traveling backward while reversing the chain. This time the person holding the hoop steps backward through it first.

- The "ring on a chain" movement is also created with a human chain, but this time students hold hands and form a circle (figure 9.46b). Without letting go of hands, try to move a hoop around the circle back to its starting point.

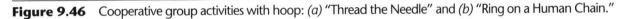

Figure 9.46   Cooperative group activities with hoop: *(a)* "Thread the Needle" and *(b)* "Ring on a Human Chain."

Ribbon Skills

Ribbons are unique to the sport of rhythmic gymnastics. The first time they hold a ribbon, students will naturally wave it in the air to create interesting shapes and patterns. Encourage this exploration so that students will begin to feel connected to the movement of the ribbon rather than observe its actions independently. Ribbons are compelling apparatus and can be as expressive as the students holding them. The movement of the student and the ribbon blend with the music, like poetry in motion.

As explained in chapter 2, ribbons should be long enough to create and sustain a pattern but short enough to maneuver. For younger children, ribbons should be 3.5 meters. Older students can typically handle a ribbon up to 5 meters in length. Students will experience greater success and will be less likely to become entangled with the ribbon when provided with a ribbon of appropriate length, and when provided with some coaching on basic technique.

For safety, the ribbon stick should always be grasped with the end of the stick in the palm of the hand. The index finger can rest along the length of the stick to help control its movement. Figure 9.47 shows this proper grip. Children have a tendency to grab the stick in the middle, with the handle poking out, creating the possibility of endangering themselves or other students. Stick safety should be reviewed before every ribbon lesson.

Figure 9.47   Grip on the ribbon stick.

Before performing beginning ribbon skills, students should have developed good general and personal spatial awareness, because their personal space has now been enlarged with the addition of a stick in their hands. A large area is needed to perform ribbon skills and movements safely. Partner skills are more difficult to perform with the ribbon. A few suggestions for group work are included at the end of this section. These focus on the use of the ribbon with other apparatus. Ribbon skills (or fundamental elements) can be divided into the following categories:

- Swing
- Circle
- Figure 8
- Spiral (or corkscrew)
- Snake

▶ Swings

Figure 9.48   Swings with the ribbon: front and side plane.

Swings are one of the easiest skills to perform with the ribbon and should be taught first. During a swing motion, the ribbon creates a half circle. The swinging motion comes from the shoulder and is a smooth, continuous motion. Swings can be performed in frontal, sagittal, and horizontal planes (figure 9.48).

Teaching Tips

- The arm should swing in a relaxed pendulum motion.
- Swings are a natural progression to circles.
- Swings are great connecting moves to other skills.
- Widen the stance during front swings to attain full reach with the body as the weight transfers from one foot to the other.
- The ribbon stick should become a straight extension of the arm.
- Try to keep the ribbon silent; avoid cracks and snaps.

Learning Challenges

- Show a swing on both sides of the body. Try to move the ribbon from the right to the left hand smoothly. Then try switching hands at the bottom and at the top of the swing. Which way works better?
- Swing in time to a piece of music. As the music increases in tempo, so should the speed of the swing.

- Show a swing at the front, back, and sides of the body. Use both right and left hands.
- Swing across the front of the body at the level of the horizon as if you are making yourself a large tummy.
- When performing a swing in front of the body, try to step over the ribbon. Keep swinging and stepping over the ribbon as you move forward.
- Try a swing in back of the body and step backward over the ribbon.
- Create swing patterns (e.g., swing on the right two times, change hands, swing on the left two times, swing across the front using both hands).
- Swing the ribbon and then turn the body to change the orientation of the swing. From a front swing, turning a quarter turn will create a side swing. (If the stick is in the right hand, it is easier to turn a quarter turn to the left.)
- Create a combination of swings and circles (e.g., swing, swing, circle, swing, swing, circle).
- Perform a swing and add locomotion to travel across the gym (e.g., front swings with side steps, front swings with crossover steps, side swings with forward hops).

▶ Circles

After learning and practicing swings with the ribbon, circles are a natural progression. When performing circles, the arm is fully extended and straight but not stiff. The circling motion is initiated from the shoulder. The ribbon should stay in motion and not drag or fall on the floor.

Teaching Tips

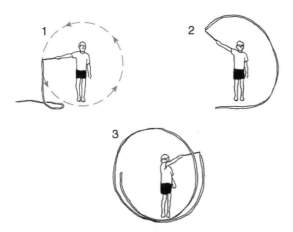

- Circles should stay in one of the three planes: frontal, sagittal (side), or horizontal (overhead).
- Watch the circle shape made by the ribbon and try to make the shape more round by adjusting the arm's movement.
- Check stick length to ensure that the ribbon stick will not be hitting the floor during front or side circles.
- To improve front circles, stand a few inches from and facing a wall. Then perform a circle so that the ribbon stick lightly touches the wall.
- Try a circle and a half pattern as illustrated in figure 9.49.

Figure 9.49   Circle and a half with ribbon.

Learning Challenges

- Try creating circles in the frontal plane, in the sagittal plane, and in the horizontal plane (figure 9.50). Then try creating circles overhead and on the ground in front of the body (as though drawing a large circle on the floor).

| Horizontal | Sagittal | Frontal |

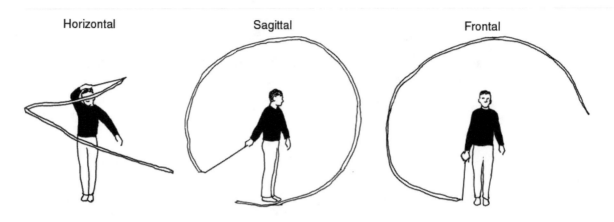

Figure 9.50   Ribbon circles in three planes: Horizontal (overhead); sagittal (side), and frontal.

- Show an overhead circle and then change the level of the body and the circle (e.g., stand while performing overhead circles, then crouch down to a kneeling position, then stand up again, and so on). Be sure to maintain the circle shape while changing levels.

- Show a circle and try to step into the circle or over the ribbon (e.g., perform a side circle, and as the ribbon stick passes the leg, step over the ribbon with that leg).

- Create a circle on the floor in front of the body and find a way to jump in and out of the ribbon circle without getting tangled.

▶ Figure 8s

The figure 8 is simply the action of combining two circles into a single pattern. The sagittal figure 8 is the easiest to begin with when using the ribbon. The arm creates a single circle on one side of the body followed by a circle on the other side of the body.

Teaching Tips

- Figure 8 patterns are a more advanced skill. Students around the ages of 6–10 can master a basic figure 8 pattern as it simply entails drawing an 8 on its side (lazy 8) using the ribbon. A true sagittal figure 8 is simply the linking of circles on each side of the body—still a relatively easy skill to master. The horizontal figure 8 is a more advanced skill suitable for children aged 9 and older. Children may readily discover the sagittal figure 8 on their own, however the horizontal figure 8 is more abstract and may require direct teaching.

- Explain what a figure 8 pattern looks like by using the arms to draw the shape in the air.

- Explore figure 8 patterns with a scarf or a folded rope to reinforce the concept.

- A figure 8 with the ribbon is two circles joined together with a change of plane or direction.

Learning Challenges

Figure 9.51   Side figure 8.

- Draw a figure 8 on its side (lazy 8) by moving an arm through the air. Then try the same motion with the ribbon to see how the ribbon duplicates the figure 8 pattern.

- Create a circle on one side of the body followed by a circle on the other side of the body. This is a side (sagittal) figure 8 pattern (figure 9.51). Try changing hands. When performing a circle on the left side, use the right hand; when performing a circle on the right side, use the left hand.

- Draw a horizontal figure 8 by creating a circle on the floor in front of the body and then connecting it to an overhead circle (figure 9.52). (This is a more advanced skill that will require direct teaching.)

- After mastering the horizontal figure 8 pattern, try holding the end of the ribbon with the free hand and creating the figure 8. (Note: The hand holding the ribbon must participate in the figure 8 pattern or it will get tangled.)

- Try a side (sagittal) figure 8 and step over the ribbon as it passes one side of the body (figure 9.53).

- Try all the figure 8 patterns using the "other" hand.

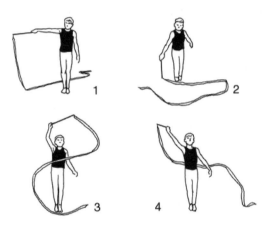

Figure 9.52   Horizontal figure 8 with ribbon.

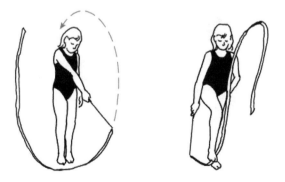

Figure 9.53   Figure 8, incorporating stepping over the ribbon.

▶ Spirals

After exploring circles, students can move on to the spiraling motion of the ribbon, which is a series of tight small circles. A circle uses the entire arm, but the tight circles of a spiral are initiated from the wrist, which creates small and fast circles. Spirals can be performed with an inward or outward motion, in all planes, and are easily combined with locomotion and balances.

Teaching Tips

- Keep the arm up and the stick pointing down to avoid tangles.
- Involve the entire ribbon in the spiral; there should be no sagging tails!
- Initiate the spiral motion from the wrist. If students try to use their arms, the ribbon will likely become tangled.

Learning Challenges

- Create a spiral in front of the body and travel backward to keep the ribbon off the floor. Try using different types of locomotion when traveling backward.
- Spiral across the body and back again. Switch hands. Try to switch hands as smoothly as possible.
- Spiral the ribbon and perform a body turn. Try turning at all three levels (i.e., high, medium, and low).
- Invent three new balances, and try to maintain the spiral while moving from one balance to the next.
- Spiral across the front of the body and then complete a front circle, followed by more spirals. Try to keep the pattern going.
- Perform small spirals on the ribbon while travelling backwards. Gradually increase the size of the spirals until they become large frontal circles (figure 9.54).

Figure 9.54   Examples of ribbon spirals.

▶ Snakes

Snakes with the ribbon are sometimes known as serpents. Often children like to call them "waves." The snake motion of the ribbon is an easy skill for everyone to master. Like the spiral, the snake motion is initiated from the wrist in a tight side-to-side or up-and-down motion. Snakes also combine well with locomotion skills and balances.

Teaching Tips

- Keep the arm up and the stick pointing down to avoid tangles.
- Involve the entire ribbon in the snake movement.
- A well-executed snake has four to five even bends of the ribbon.
- The snake motion is generated from the wrist.
- There are two kinds of snakes (figure 9.55):
  - The vertical snake is like waving good-bye; the wrist performs an up-and-down motion.
  - The frontal snake is like a pendulum; the wrist performs a side-to-side motion.

Pendulum   Vertical

Figure 9.55 Types of snakes: pendulum and vertical.

Learning Challenges

- Explore snake patterns from a kneeling position (figure 9.56). Shoot the ribbon out in front of and snake it back toward the body, like a snake in the grass. Then have the ribbon snake across in front of the body, like a sea serpent going in and out of the waves.
- Travel forward and let the ribbon snake behind the back. Keep the end of the stick pointing downward so that the ribbon does not tangle.

Figure 9.56 Snake patterns on the ground from a kneeling position.

- Snake the ribbon on the floor and run over ribbon each time it passes in front of the feet (figure 9.57). Start out slow, then increase speed.

- Jump up and let the ribbon go behind the back. Then snake it downward.

Partner and Group Work

Partner and group work, because of its interactive nature, is inadvisable with the ribbon because children should be encouraged to use their ribbons safely in their own space. Having students work side by side to create beautiful group performances with the ribbon can encourage group interaction, however. Older students, who are exploring partner relationships in more depth, might enjoy combining ribbon skills with hoop skills because they complement each other in a routine.

Figure 9.57   Stepping over snakes on the floor.

- Using a ribbon and a hoop, have one person spiral the ribbon. The second person holds the hoop while the ribbon person steps into it. The hoop person then carefully guides the hoop up and around the ribbon person and their ribbon, without interfering with the spiraling action of the ribbon (figure 9.58).

Figure 9.58   Ribbon combined with hoop.

- Facing each other, students hold their ribbons in their right hands. They face each other and grasp the ribbon of their partner (where it joins the stick) with their left hands. While walking backwards they let their partners ribbon travel through their hands as they stretch the ribbon into two parallel lines until the reach the end of the ribbon. The ribbons can then be lowered and raise or students can create small waves while sill holding on to their partner's ribbon.

Scarf Skills

Scarves are a beautiful and *quiet* rhythmic gymnastics apparatus that are fun for all. Although not considered "official" rhythmic gymnastics apparatus, scarves are indispensable within a rhythmic gymnastics program. Rhythmic gymnastics scarves may be handheld, juggling-type scarves, or one large, flowing scarf. The small handheld scarves work especially well for younger children.

Students love to wave and throw scarves. The natural, gently flowing nature of scarves lends itself well to slow and graceful rhythmic movement. Multitudes of throwing and catching activities for handheld scarves are excellent for developing hand-eye coordination. These activities are also good for beginners. After being thrown the scarves float gently downward, leaving children ample time to catch them before they hit the floor. The imaginative play that evolves from scarf exploration with young children is especially fun to watch and older children love the challenge of trying to juggle three small scarves at a time.

The elements for the scarf are similar to ribbon skills. Be sure to allow young students to explore using small scarves before moving onto ribbon skills, however. To ensure immediate success with scarf activities, ensure that the scarf material is very light—that is, it should flow up and through the air effortlessly. Scarf skills can be divided into the following fundamental element categories:

- Swing
- Circle
- Wave
- Figure 8
- Throw and catch

The scarf can be held it many different ways. Large scarves can be held along the long edge or the short edge. The large scarf can be grasped from one corner or two opposing corners. For small handheld scarves, the corners are lightly grasped between the thumb and forefinger, enabling the forefinger to guide the scarf's movement.

▶ Swings

Swings are the fundamental element common to every rhythmic gymnastics apparatus. Performing swings with a scarf is a very basic movement but one that is visually pleasing. The movement should be soft and gentle, and it should involve the entire body, not just the arms. Swings with the scarf progress to full circles.

Teaching Tips

- Use music to inspire natural and flowing swings.
- Use one or two small scarves or one large scarf to begin.

Learning Challenges

- Play music with a definite but gentle beat. Swing the scarf from side to side or from front to back. When the music stops, hold the position. When the music continues, continue swinging (figure 9.59).

Figure 9.59 Swings with small scarves.

- Swing the scarf from side to side. Move the arms forward and backward in unison or in opposition (i.e., one arm goes forward while the other arm swings backward).
- Play skipping music and try to skip holding the scarves. The arms swing at the sides in time to the music.

▶ Circles

Scarf circles performed in the frontal plane are easier and should therefore be taught first. Simply draw a circular shape using a scarf like paint on a canvas. Circles can be performed in the frontal plane clockwise and counterclockwise. They can be performed in the side (sagittal) plane together, one after the other, or in syncopation.

Teaching Tips

- Circles can be large or small.
- Circles can be done with one or two scarves in all three planes (i.e., frontal, horizontal, and sagittal).

Learning Challenges

- Show a scarf circle in each of the planes—frontal, horizontal, and sagittal. Use one or two scarves (figure 9.60).

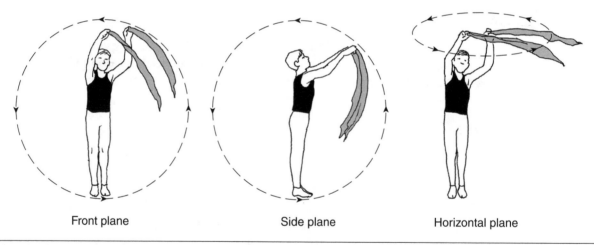

Front plane   Side plane   Horizontal plane

Figure 9.60   Circles with scarf in three different planes.

- With a small scarf in each hand, travel backward and show backward arm circles. Then travel forward while showing forward arm circles. At the signal, stop and freeze. Now try the reverse (i.e., travel backward when doing forward arm circles and travel forward when doing backward arm circles). (This activity will challenge students' ability to think while moving.)

• Complete a circle with one or two scarves. At the height of the circle, release the scarf (or scarves); then catch the scarf and continue the circle (figure 9.61).

Figure 9.61 Combining a sagittal circle with a throw.

► Waves

Waves with scarves describe the up-and-down or side-to-side motion of scarves. The action can be initiated by the wrist, very similar to the action used to create a snake using the ribbon, or by a large movement of the arms for a large wave pattern.

Teaching Tips

• A wave is similar to waving a hand.
• Waves can be done with two handheld scarves or by holding the corners of a large scarf.

Learning Challenges

• Wave two small scarves when traveling backward. At the signal, throw the scarves into the air in front of the body, catch them, and continue traveling backward. Find a different way to travel backward whenever throwing and catching.
• Create a sequence using waves and levels (e.g., short and small waves at a low level, fast alternating waves at a medium level, and long and tall waves at a high level; figure 9.62).

Figure 9.62 Sequence of waves at different levels.

- Imagine being in a glass room and use the scarves to "polish the glass."
- Combine a turning movement with waves (e.g., pivot turn, three-step turn).
- Show a large wave using a large scarf (figure 9.63). Holding the scarf in two hands behind the back, lunge forward and wave the scarf forward. Then step back and pull the scarf backward overhead.

Figure 9.63   Large wave with a large scarf.

▶ Figure 8s

A figure 8 is two circles joined together with a change of plane or direction. The figure 8 pattern with the scarf is similar to the same fundamental element using the ribbon. Students create it by drawing an 8 in the air (the scarf will mimic the arm's movement).

Teaching Tips

- The figure 8 pattern can be performed in the horizontal and vertical planes.
- Figure 8s can be executed with one hand or both hands.
- Using a large scarf will help students master the more complex horizontal figure 8.

Learning Challenges

- Holding a scarf, draw a figure 8 pattern on its side. Then draw a figure 8 that is standing up (figure 9.64). When "crazy 8s" is called, make the scarf do a figure 8 pattern anywhere.

- Perform a horizontal figure 8 (figure 9.65). (It is easiest to teach a horizontal figure 8 with imagery using a large scarf.) Hold a large scarf, along the long edge, in front of you between two outstretched arms. Swing the scarf around to one side like you are putting on a large cape so that the scarf is behind your back. One hand will be circling overhead while the other will be staying at shoulder height. Take the cape off the other side of the body until it is held out in front again. Repeat this movement without letting the scarf touch the body and without stopping and you will have completed a horizontal figure 8.

Figure 9.64   Examples of two figure 8 patterns with a scarf.

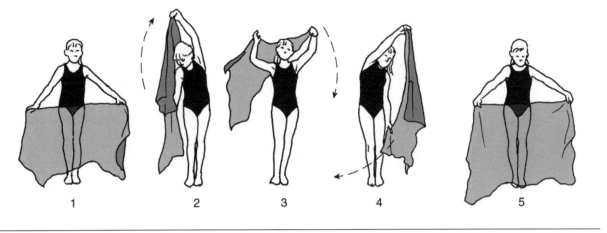

Figure 9.65 Horizontal figure 8.

- Perform a "butterfly," a beautiful rhythmic gymnastics movement that is simply two vertical figure 8s side by side (figure 9.66). With a scarf in each hand, simultaneously draw the figure 8 pattern. Exaggerate the movement to give the scarf extra lift. Try the same pattern holding the corners of a large scarf.

Figure 9.66 Butterfly movement with two scarves.

Throws and Catches

Because scarves are soft and float through the air, they are usually easy to catch. Thus, throws and catches are basic skills that can be performed by all students. Throws with scarves are also visually effective, allowing students to perform a body movement while the scarf is in the air.

Teaching Tips

- Throwing and catching with scarves is fun and easy because there is ample reaction time.
- For extra challenge, use small scarves for juggling.
- Try to keep the scarves away from the body to allow them to flow freely.

Learning Challenges

- Throw and catch small scarves in a variety of ways (e.g., throw with one hand and catch with both hands; throw with the left hand and catch with the right; throw two scarves into the air and cross them before catching; hold a static position when catching). Create other throws and catches.

- Hold a large scarf by two corners along the shorter edge. Travel backward and wave the scarf up and down. Then stop, throw the scarf corners behind the back, and grasp the other two corners (figure 9.67).

Figure 9.67   Wave and throw with a large scarf.

Figure 9.68   Three-scarf juggle.

- Juggle three different-colored scarves (figure 9.68). (This is a favorite activity with older students and is fairly easy to master.)

Summary

Using apparatus in fun and creative ways is the ultimate goal of any rhythmic gymnastics program. By proceeding through the learning challenges in this chapter, students will gain experience in the fundamental movements of each apparatus: the ball, the rope, the hoop, the ribbon, and the scarf. They will also gain an understanding of the fundamental movements common to several apparatus, as in the case of swings and circles. Students will understand that they should use their entire bodies in each movement, letting the apparatus become an extension of the body rather than treating it as a moving, handheld prop. With a solid understanding of the basic skills in rhythmic gymnastics, your students are now equipped to demonstrate that understanding by creating their own sequences and routines, which is the topic of the next and final chapter in this book.

Chapter 10

© Helen Scott Studios

Routines and Beyond

After exploring and creating different movements based on the fundamenal elements for each apparatus, your students will be eager to pull all they have learned into a sequence or routine. Skill development is the important starting point of a rhythmic gymnastics unit. Once learned, two or three skills can be linked together to form a sequence. The transition from one skill to the next should not seem obvious or deliberate in a sequence. Rather, skills should flow together smoothly and be linked logically. Sequences are an excellent way to consolidate skill practice in an interesting way. Practicing a sequence helps students solidify their skill understanding and memory, and prepares them for complete routines, which are simply created by connecting two or more sequences.

Chapter 9 has provided you with several learning challenges for each of the fundamental elements for each apparatus. Your students will have created their own ideas and movements as an extension of their learning. When these skills are brought together in a cohesive sequence or routine, the resulting product, the choreography, is something worth celebrating and acknowledging. Your students may wish to continue to refine and develop their routine in order to share it with a wider audience. This chapter will provide suggestions for selecting music and the apparatus that is appropriate for the music and the students. The skills selected for inclusion into the routine are important too, as they should be within the ability of each group member as well as show variety. Good routine choreography will include a change of tempo in the routine, use of both sides of the body, dynamic and energetic movements along with good use of the floor area. The latter part of this chapter discusses how to help your student prepare for the big performance. Students should be encouraged to show amplitude and expression when performing their routine. The final part of the chapter outlines some key points to consider in the final presentation such as sound system, venue, and entrances and exits.

Choreographing a Routine or Sequence

Choreography is creating a sequence by linking skills together. Students can create their own routine choreography independently, or with limited suggestions and assistance from you. Or, you may want to prescribe a sequence or two to get them started on routine creation. Routine-planning posters are helpful at this point in the rhythmic gymnastics unit (see appendix). Proper record keeping is important when planning routines because it helps students remember their routines in the proper sequence. Refer once again to figure 3.2 for a routine-planning form. Having a set routine plan also helps students to practice their sequences in the same way at each practice, which in turn assists with the memorization process. I have observed older students create and memorize sequences with more than a dozen skills!

In addition to beautiful and visually captivating choreography, the music and its suitability to the apparatus used must also be considered. In the next section, we'll discuss how to select the proper music for any routine.

Music

The foundation of a good routine is selecting suitable musical accompaniment. Choose music that is appealing and appropriate for the age of your students. For younger children choose music with an audible beat. This will help them hear the tempo and rhythm in the music. A selection of familiar childhood favorites will probably not be well received by a group of middle school students, but they might be inspired by some retro music from a past era or by current favorites. Be sure that selected music contains lyrics that are appropriate and not overly sophisticated. That is, lyrics should not be overly suggestive or vulgar. (Of course, if you stick to instrumental music, you won't have to worry about inappropriate lyrics.)

The most difficult part of music selection is finding a piece of music that suits the chosen apparatus. A skipping routine will work best with an upbeat tempo. A ribbon routine will necessitate music with smooth, flowing rhythms. When listening to potential music selections simply try to visualize the type of apparatus that might best suit that particular piece of music.

Also enlist the help of your students in music selection. I typically find three appropriate pieces of music and edit them to a shorter length. Then, when student groups are working in the gym, I have each group listen to each piece (or shortened clip) of music and select the song they like the best for their chosen routine. During routine practice, I play the same three pieces of music, one after another. The students continue working on their routines even when their music is not playing, but when their song is played they have the opportunity to practice their routine to the music. This is an excellent way to save yourself the time of having to organize seven or eight pieces of music for student groups. (It also eliminates the noise of seven or eight songs being played in the gym at one time.)

The length of each music selection will likely have to be shortened for younger students. The following guidelines will help you to decide on what is an appropriate routine length for each age group.

Age (years)	Time
5 – 7	30 seconds – 1 minute
7 – 10	1 – 1.5 minutes
10 – 12	1.5 – 2.0 minutes
12 and up	2.0 – 3.5 minutes

When selecting music length for a routine, be sure to consider how many skills will be included within the entire routine. It's also a good idea to put yourself in the shoes of audience members, asking yourself whether this performance piece will hold their interest. If not, you may want to shorten the routine.

Apparatus

Choosing apparatus is another important step in choreography. The chosen apparatus should be suitable for the age group of your students. Small scarves are visually exciting and are appropriate for young children. Longer ribbons are more appropriate for older students, who will be better able to keep them flowing and prevent tangles. If the routine will be performed in a large venue, like an arena or a stadium, you will want to choose brightly colored apparatus that will fill the large space—for example, ribbons, scarves, or hoops.

Equipment cost and availability will also need to be considered when planning a routine. For a kindergarten volunteer celebration, we fashioned simple tambourines from two paper plates, beans, and crepe paper streamers. Outfitting the entire class with a hand apparatus was affordable in this case; the students made the tambourines in class and after the performance they were able to take them home as souvenirs of the event.

Skills

Effective choreography will also depend on selecting appropriate skills for the routine. Students should be able to complete each skill independently before putting it into a sequence or routine. Also, discourage students from using only their most advanced skills in a routine. Often the simplest movements are the most visually appealing. Overly complex sequences will look cluttered and disorganized, so keep it simple.

Variety in Movement

Include a variety of movements in every routine, both to maintain students' interest in the routine and to make the routine interesting. For example, include bounces, body and floor rolls, and throws and catches in a ball routine. For younger students, repeating a skill to complement the music is appropriate. A beginner ball routine might include a beginning balance, four two-handed bounces, four throws and catches, four rolls up and down the arm, and an ending balance.

Older students can create routines with less repetition using a variety of movements. For example, students might create the following ball routine.

A static balance

Followed by a series of rhythmic bounces

Then a throw from the standing position and

A catch at a low level

Then a body roll on the ball at a low level

Followed by a throw from a low level

Then rise to a high level and catch

Exchange with a partner (rolls and throws)

Roll the ball around the legs in a figure 8 pattern

Pick up the ball in a final static position.

Similar skills can be performed at different levels to help maintain interest and to continually challenge students. A more complex ball skill, for example, might be bouncing the ball with one hand and then changing levels while sustaining a bouncing rhythm.

Also important is the way different moves and skills are connected. The routine should be fluid. That is, one movement should flow into the next, as opposed to a simple display of several, unconnected skills. Although smooth transitions from one skill to the next are sometimes difficult, many movements flow logically into others. A swing, for example, turns easily into a circle and can be done with a ball, scarf, ribbon, and hoop. In short, the more variety in the routine, the more appealing it will be.

Change of Tempo

A well-choreographed routine will often include a change in tempo to add variety and interest. One of the easiest ways to do this is to find a piece of music that has a change of tempo in the arrangement. Then the movements can be chosen to suit the music. Another way, of course, is to edit two pieces of music together. Sometimes, however, a change of tempo is not needed—remember that younger students will often benefit from the predictability of a steady, even beat and tempo.

Body Symmetry

Body symmetry is using both sides of the body equally. In rhythmic gymnastics, students should be encouraged to use both hands to manipulate an apparatus. To facilitate this you can simply ask them to perform a skill on one side and then on the other side. Using both sides of the body in routines will not only produce well-balanced, attractive, and visually appealing routines but also help to increase students' coordination. And, by including both right and left hand movements in routine choreography, students will be actively exercising both sides of their bodies during practice.

Dynamic Movements

When students work with apparatus they sometimes become so focused on manipulating the apparatus that they forget about body movements. Thus, to produce a dynamic movement, they will sometimes need to be encouraged to allow their bodies to become more involved (along with the apparatus) in the movement. In a good rhythmic gymnastics routine or sequence the apparatus should look like an extension of the body, not simply a moving piece of gymnastics equipment. Involvement of the entire body in the movement adds to a routine's aesthetic appeal. (It also promotes fitness.) Dynamic movements help to give the sequence or routine energy and life.

Floor Coverage

Students may need to be encouraged to move around the gym and utilize more floor space by adding locomotion movements. Help them to "cover the floor" by reminding them about pathways and direction. If a group is preparing for a performance, there are many ways they can organize themselves in different formations such as half-circles, staggered lines or diagonal lines; figure 10.1 shows diagrams of group formations. Also consider the venue in which they will be performing. Where should the performers be situated so that the audience will get the best view of the performance?

Facing the audience at the front

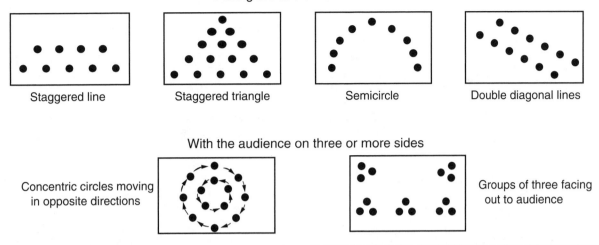

| Staggered line | Staggered triangle | Semicircle | Double diagonal lines |

With the audience on three or more sides

Concentric circles moving in opposite directions

Groups of three facing out to audience

Figure 10.1 Examples of group formations for performances or displays.

Group Work Dynamics

Variety and interest can be added to group routines in several ways. Students can use different apparatus within a routine. Some combinations that work well are hoop and ball, ribbon and hoop, and ball and ribbon. Innovative use of equipment will also emerge as students discover how they can relate the two apparatus into a movement pattern. For example, one group member holds the hoop out horizontally while the second group member bounces a ball in the hoop. In addition, group members can exchange equipment during a routine to add visual interest. Apparatus can be exchange by throwing, rolling, sliding, and passing.

To add variety to a routine, one group member can show free body movements (i.e., no apparatus) while other group members manipulate two pieces of equipment (e.g., two ribbons). Students can also explore partner relationships by varying the manner in which they interact during a routine. For example, performing a skill in canon (i.e., the first person performs a skill, followed immediately by subsequent students performing the same skill) is a way that students can interact within a routine to add variety and interest.

Variety is also achieved by highlighting individual performances within the larger group performance. For example, the group performs the beginning part of a routine. Partway through, individuals break apart from the

group to perform two or three skills each. Then for the end of the routine, the group comes back together. Group members can also try different formations. Transitioning from formation to formation will be a good challenge for older students. Some examples of formation changes are shown in figure 10.2.

Routine creation is a fun process for students. They are able to bring much of what they have learned into creating a cohesive sequence of movements. As educators, we have come to understand that the process of arriving at the product is sometimes more important than the product itself. In a rhythmic gymnastics unit the process (i.e., discovering and learning new skills) and the product (i.e., putting the skills into routines and sequences) are equally important. Creating an entire rhythmic gymnastics routine is satisfying for both students and teachers. It is a celebration of individual accomplishments and the learning that has occurred during the rhythmic gymnastics unit. The opportunity to perform with confidence in front of others, be it a large or small group, can be a most rewarding and satisfying experience.

Refining the Finished Routine

Your students have arrived at the point where they are able to create rhythmic gymnastics

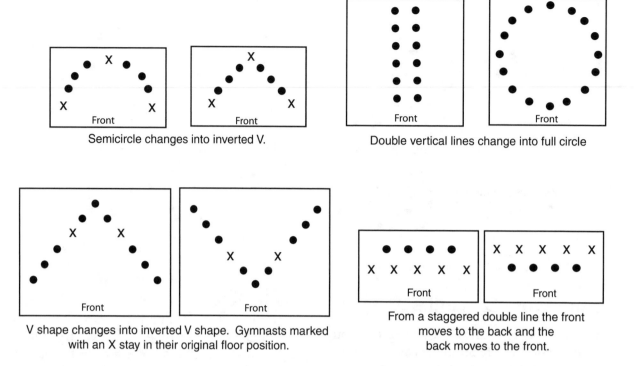

Semicircle changes into inverted V.

Double vertical lines change into full circle

V shape changes into inverted V shape. Gymnasts marked with an X stay in their original floor position.

From a staggered double line the front moves to the back and the back moves to the front.

Figure 10.2   Examples of group formation transitions for performances or displays.

routines and sequences using a variety of skills. They have demonstrated skill mastery within the routines and sequences and they may be using different levels, planes, pathways, and tempo changes. They also understand the importance of using both sides of their bodies and how to cover a large floor area to add interest and variety to their routines. Now is the time to help them develop and refine their routines to create as visually appealing and aesthetically pleasing a performance as possible. You will want to encourage amplitude in your students —that is, to perform skills with a full extension of the body and the apparatus. Try to encourage your students to be expressive with their movements and their bodies by showing energy and enjoyment during their performances. Prior to the actual performance it would be helpful to provide your students with tips for refining their performance skills.

Amplitude

When students perform rhythmic gymnastics skills, both free movements and skills with apparatus, amplitude can add a lot to the aesthetics of a performance. Amplitude is most simply described as full use of the body, limbs, and apparatus during a movement. In other words, the arms should extend fully, with attention paid to hand position. The legs should be fully extended, right down to the foot and ankle. And full range of motion should be used in all joints to gain maximum amplitude.

Amplitude can best be demonstrated with a ribbon. While holding the ribbon, show a circle in front of your body using only your forearm (below the elbow). Then perform the same circle using your entire arm, from the shoulder joint, to demonstrate a full range of motion and a large circle. Performing a routine with good amplitude gives the routine more energy and life.

Expression

Expression is the ability to convey an idea or emotion through movement. Effective expression in rhythmic gymnastics often comes with maturity and experience. Some students are naturally expressive in their faces and with their bodies. When they perform a skill or routine they seem to come to life. Energy and enthusiasm also play a large part in expression. When students are enjoying moving to music and sharing their newly discovered skills and talents, they seem to exude a natural energy.

Music can "draw out" feeling and emotion in a routine. When students kinesthetically feel music it translates into their presentation. Just turn on a piece of funky or energetic music and ask a group of children to move to the music. Their bodies literally translate the music through movement. To encourage expressive movement, do everything you can to support students during the exploration and discovery process. When students feel this unconditional support, they will be more likely to summon their innately expressive natures.

Presentation Skills

If your students will be presenting their routines to a large audience or at a special event, assembly, or other learning celebration, you will want to help them prepare by offering some tips on presentation. Students should be well prepared and have their routines memorized, of course, but it may be helpful to teach them some strategies to use if they suddenly forget parts of their routines. They may need to watch another student to catch up. They may need to listen for certain cues in the music to figure out where they are in the routine. Or, they may simply need to cover up a mistake by ad-libbing.

In addition, spend some time on the following presentation skills.

- Show students how to develop a relationship with their audience by establishing eye contact, or at the very least projecting their eyesight forward and upward.
- Students will need practice with spacing and synchronization. Show them how to watch the person to the side of them by using peripheral vision.

- Students will need to practice performing the skills together so that their movements are synchronous. Part of the visual excitement of rhythmic gymnastics is when a large group performs movements simultaneously and in unison.
- Encourage students to practice in the performance venue to orient their spacing on the floor. Also be sure that students know where they will enter and where they will exit at the start and end of their routines.
- Color and uniformity also add to a group performance. You may want to suggest that students wear similar clothing. This need not be an additional expense. In lieu of similar clothing or color, you might simply require that everyone wear a brightly colored top with dark shorts.
- The best performance tip you can offer your students is to simply go out and have fun. If students can share their excitement for movement, their performance will surely be a success.

Assessing the Finished Routine

Bringing student learning to the point where the students are performing their skills within a routine can be very satisfying. Students will have seen a project through to completion from the beginning stages of discovery and creating through the process of collaborating to put the skills together. With the final goal being met, that of putting all the skills together in a routine performed for the enjoyment of others, children gain tremendous satisfaction.

The questions in figure 10.3 can be used as a checklist and will help you assess the performance of student sequences and routines as well as their ability to work with others in a collaborative setting.

Group name:

Members:

1   2   3   (1 = Excellent; 2 = Satisfactory; 3 = Improvement needed)

_____   Did the students follow the guidelines provided?

_____   Did students cooperate and collaborate within their group?

_____   Did the students choose skills that were safe and perform them safely?

_____   Were the skills identifiable within the sequence or routine?

_____   Were transitions between skills smooth and fluid?

_____   Was the routine visually appealing?

_____   Were different pathways, levels, planes, and directions used to add variety and interest?

_____   Did the movements reflect the tempo, beat, and mood of the music?

_____   Did the group show a change in formation?

Comments:

Figure 10.3   Teacher assessment checklist for a routine or sequence.
From *Teaching Rhythmic Gymnastics: A Developmentally Appropriate Approach* by Heather Palmer, 2003, Champaign, IL: Human Kinetics.

Planning the Performance

A large group performance can be a wonderful way to celebrate a school rally, sport competition, or other special event. To ensure a successful performance, there are a number of elements to consider. The following pre-performance checklist will help you "cover all the bases" and ensure that you and your students are ready for the big performance.

- Is the venue large enough for the performers to move safely?
- Is there adequate seating for the audience?

- Do fire codes or other restrictions limit the number of people in the audience or in the performance venue?
- Will the ceiling height permit free movement of the chosen apparatus?
- Is the audience a safe enough distance from the performers (i.e., in case an apparatus goes astray)?
- Does the sound system project music clearly and audibly?
- Are the entrances and exits clear of obstacles?
- Is there an extra copy of the performance music available as back up?
- Will students have the opportunity to warm up prior to their performance?

Summary

Once a solid foundation has been established, the fun really begins. That is, once students have learned the skills and developed them fully, they can exercise their creativity, pulling together the skills and movements and creating short sequences or longer routines. Good routine choreography will depend on a number of factors. Appropriate music selection is essential. The music should suit the age of participants and the chosen apparatus. If possible, find music that has a change of tempo so that the routine does not become monotonous. Also be creative when selecting equipment and try new apparatus for variety.

The skills that are included in choreographed routines should be simple movement patterns that fall within the skill ability of the group. These skills should show variety to make sequences and routines interesting for both the participants and the audience. Students will need to be encouraged to use both sides of their bodies and to use full range of motion. Choreography for older students will involve moving across the floor instead of staying glued to one spot. Interaction between group members through apparatus exchange and change of formation will add variety and interest to the routine.

To prepare students for a performance, make sure they know their routines well before taking them to a large audience at a school assembly or special event. Once they have their routines memorized, help them begin to develop performance skills, such as showing expression, amplitude, and energy. The joy of movement and rhythmic gymnastics should be shared whenever possible. The visual effects of the apparatus are beautiful, and students will enjoy sharing what they have learned. Sit back and try to relax as your students share their love of performing and their love of rhythmic gymnastics.

Appendix
Routine-Planning Posters

There are many uses for the routine-planning posters included in the appendix. Copy them as they are or enlarge the posters to 11 by 17 inches on a copier. Laminate them and post them around the gym where students can easily see them. During stage 3, when students are learning about the fundamental movements for each apparatus, the poster can be used as a checklist. When the group identifies the fundamental element, it is checked off on the poster. The poster is a great visual reminder to children of the fundamental elements for each apparatus as they continue to create sequences and routines.

The posters are very useful when students are working on their group or individual routines. If you want each group or individual to perform routines with similar fundamental elements, you can simply check off the elements on the posters (using erasable marker) that the students should combine in a routine. To offer choices to the students, you might create a routine plan for three different apparatus and let them choose which one they wish to use for their routine. The routine plan can be as specific or as general as you wish. You might ask older students to show levels, planes, directions, or pathways in their routine; simply check off the specific movements that you would like to see them demonstrate. Also included on the routine-planning posters are body movements (e.g., pivots, leaps and jumps). Be cautious, however, about imposing too many requirements on each routine, because students will likely become more concerned with following the plan than being creative and using their imaginations to create a routine.

A third option is to provide each student or group with an original-sized copy of the poster specific to the apparatus that they have chosen for their routine. The student or group then decides which fundamental elements and body movements they plan to include in their routine. This can be a working copy for the group that changes and evolves as they work on the creation of the routine. Their final routine plan should reflect the routine that they perform for evaluative purposes.

Create a Routine Using the Ball

Use skills from the following groups:

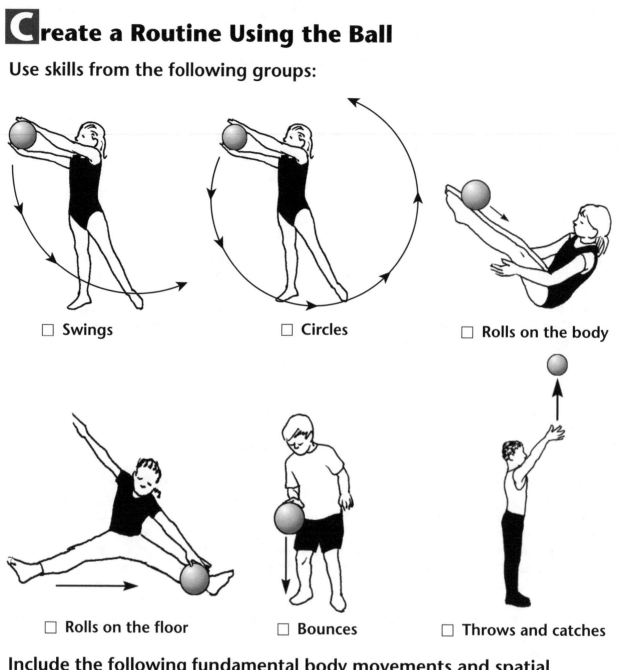

☐ Swings

☐ Circles

☐ Rolls on the body

☐ Rolls on the floor

☐ Bounces

☐ Throws and catches

Include the following fundamental body movements and spatial awareness themes:

☐ Show a beginning and ending balance.

☐ Add locomotion: skip, walk, and hop.

☐ Include a turn or a pivot.

☐ Show a jump or leap.

☐ Use both right and left hands.

☐ Show a change in tempo.

☐ Show a change of level.

☐ Try different pathways.

☐ Show a change of direction.

☐ Show different planes: sagittal (side), frontal, and horizontal.

From *Teaching Rhythmic Gymnastics: A Developmentally Appropriate Approach* by Heather Palmer, 2003, Champaign, IL: Human Kinetics.

126

Create a Routine Using the Rope

Use skills from the following groups:

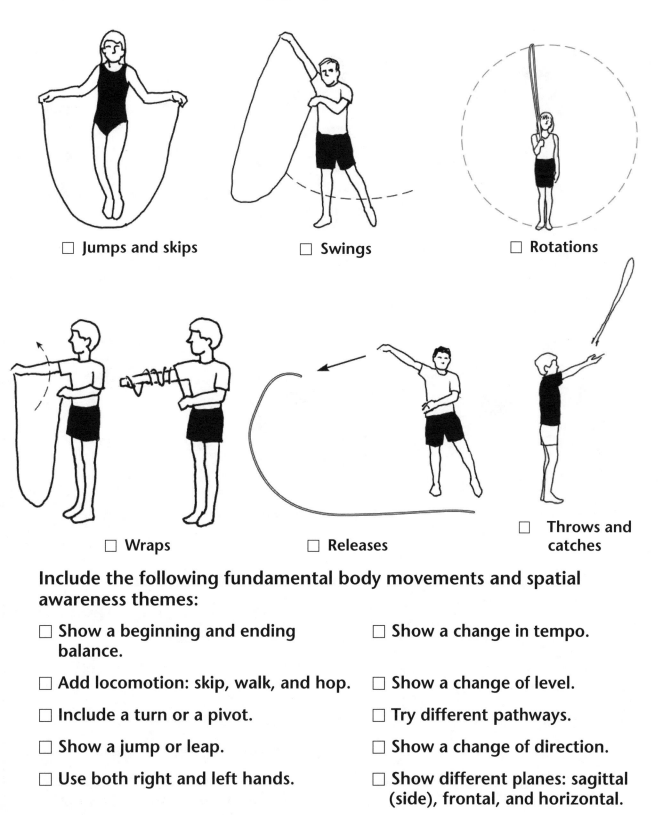

☐ Jumps and skips

☐ Swings

☐ Rotations

☐ Wraps

☐ Releases

☐ Throws and catches

Include the following fundamental body movements and spatial awareness themes:

☐ Show a beginning and ending balance.

☐ Add locomotion: skip, walk, and hop.

☐ Include a turn or a pivot.

☐ Show a jump or leap.

☐ Use both right and left hands.

☐ Show a change in tempo.

☐ Show a change of level.

☐ Try different pathways.

☐ Show a change of direction.

☐ Show different planes: sagittal (side), frontal, and horizontal.

From *Teaching Rhythmic Gymnastics: A Developmentally Appropriate Approach* by Heather Palmer, 2003, Champaign, IL: Human Kinetics.

Create a Routine Using the Hoop

Use skills from the following groups:

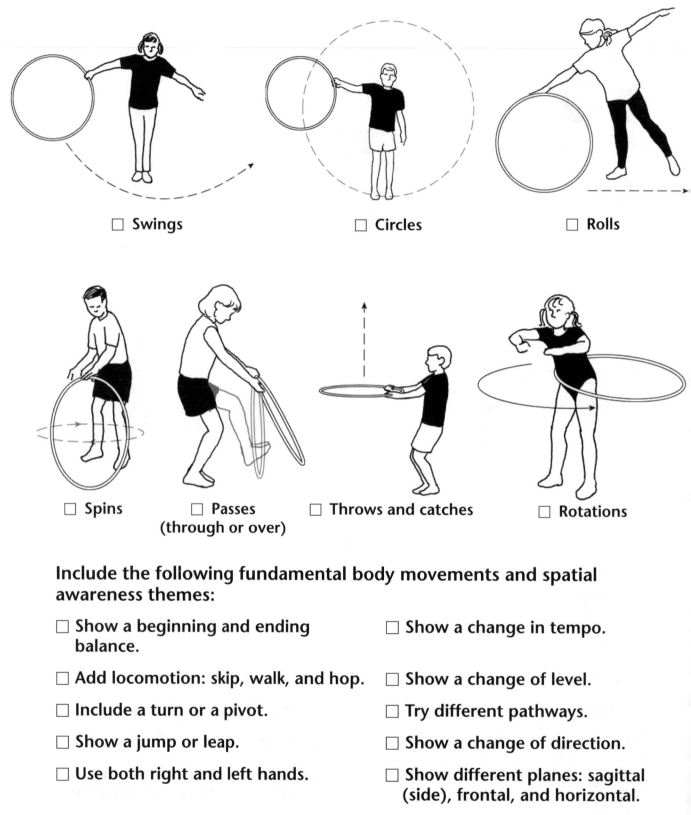

☐ Swings

☐ Circles

☐ Rolls

☐ Spins

☐ Passes
(through or over)

☐ Throws and catches

☐ Rotations

Include the following fundamental body movements and spatial awareness themes:

☐ Show a beginning and ending balance.

☐ Add locomotion: skip, walk, and hop.

☐ Include a turn or a pivot.

☐ Show a jump or leap.

☐ Use both right and left hands.

☐ Show a change in tempo.

☐ Show a change of level.

☐ Try different pathways.

☐ Show a change of direction.

☐ Show different planes: sagittal (side), frontal, and horizontal.

From *Teaching Rhythmic Gymnastics: A Developmentally Appropriate Approach* by Heather Palmer, 2003, Champaign, IL: Human Kinetics.

Create a Routine Using the Ribbon

Use skills from the following groups:

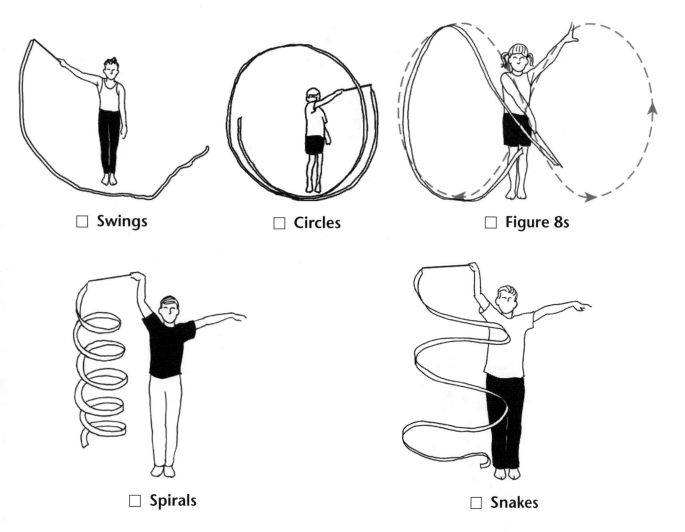

☐ Swings   ☐ Circles   ☐ Figure 8s

☐ Spirals   ☐ Snakes

Include the following fundamental body movements and spatial awareness themes:

☐ Show a beginning and ending balance.

☐ Add locomotion: skip, walk, and hop.

☐ Include a turn or a pivot.

☐ Show a jump or leap.

☐ Use both right and left hands.

☐ Show a change in tempo.

☐ Show a change of level.

☐ Try different pathways.

☐ Show a change of direction.

☐ Show different planes: sagittal (side), frontal, and horizontal.

From *Teaching Rhythmic Gymnastics: A Developmentally Appropriate Approach* by Heather Palmer, 2003, Champaign, IL: Human Kinetics.

Create a Routine Using the Scarf

Use skills from the following groups:

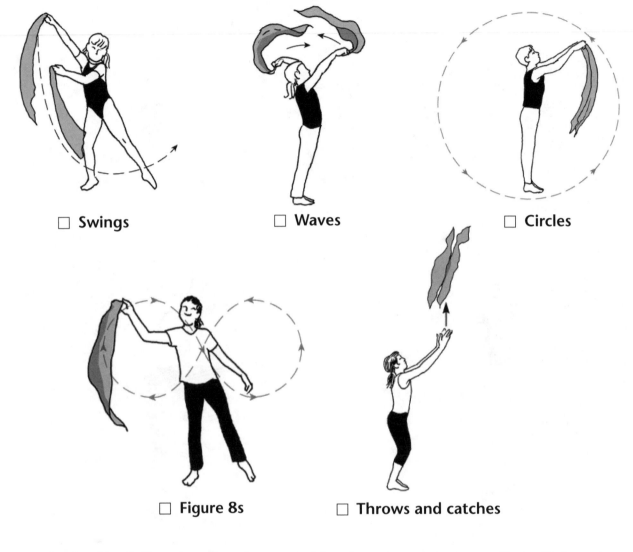

☐ Swings

☐ Waves

☐ Circles

☐ Figure 8s

☐ Throws and catches

Include the following fundamental body movements and spatial awareness themes:

☐ Show a beginning and ending balance.

☐ Add locomotion: skip, walk, and hop.

☐ Include a turn or a pivot.

☐ Show a jump or leap.

☐ Use both right and left hands.

☐ Show a change in tempo.

☐ Show a change of level.

☐ Try different pathways.

☐ Show a change of direction.

☐ Show different planes: sagittal (side), frontal, and horizontal.

From *Teaching Rhythmic Gymnastics: A Developmentally Appropriate Approach* by Heather Palmer, 2003, Champaign, IL: Human Kinetics.

About The Author

Heather C. Palmer is the program coordinator for Rhythmic Gymnastics Alberta. She discovered rhythmic gymnastics at the age of 19 (the time of her retirement from competitive artistic gymnastics), and she has been actively promoting the sport ever since.

Although she has served as a coach and judge at the competitive level, Palmer has more recently shifted her emphasis to developing rhythmic gymnastics at a recreational level. She has held numerous positions on Alberta's Provincial Rhythmic board, including coaching chair and provincial coach; the skill development program that she designed, known as PRISM, has been adopted throughout Canada. In 1992, Palmer received the Calgary Volunteer Award for developing the sport of rhythmic gymnastics in Calgary.

As a classroom teacher herself, Palmer also understands the demands of teaching. She has taught movement and rhythmic gymnastics to children throughout her teaching career. She has also taught rhythmic workshops for teachers for 12 years. She is certified as a level 3 coach in Canada's highly regarded National Coaching Certification Program and as a course conductor for level 1 and 2 technical courses in rhythmic gymnastics.

Palmer attended the 1999 World Gymnaestrada in Sweden as a team manager and hopes to attend a World Gymnaestrada as a performing gymnast. A member of the Canadian Association for Health, Physical Education, Recreation and Dance and the Coaching Association of Canada, Palmer lives in Calgary, where she teaches at Hillhurst Community School. She also runs a private club that focuses solely on recreational and performing programs. In her free time, she and her husband, Brian Unterschultz, and their two children enjoy skiing, camping, and hiking.

You'll find
other outstanding
gymnastics resources at

www.HumanKinetics.com

In the U.S. call

800-747-4457

Australia 08 8277 1555
Canada 800-465-7301
Europe .... +44 (0) 113 255 5665
New Zealand 09-523-3462

HUMAN KINETICS
The Information Leader in Physical Activity
P.O. Box 5076 • Champaign, IL 61825-5076 USA